Vol. LV No. 1
Magazine No. 218

Appalachia

Est. 1877 America's Longest-Running Journal of Mountaineering and Conservation

Appalachian Mountain Club
Boston, Massachusetts

AMC MISSION

Founded in 1876, the Appalachian Mountain Club, a nonprofit organization with more than 90,000 members, promotes the protection, enjoyment, and wise use of the mountains, rivers, and trails of the Appalachian region. We believe that the mountains and rivers have an intrinsic worth and also provide recreational opportunity, spiritual renewal, and ecological and economic health for the region. We encourage people to enjoy and appreciate the natural world because we believe that successful conservation depends on this experience.

© 2004 AMC Books

Appalachia is published by the AMC from its publications office at 5 Joy Street, Boston, Massachusetts, 02108. ISSN 0003-6587. ISBN 1-929173-59-8. Third-class postage paid at Boston, Massachusetts, and other mailing offices. The Journal is issued 2 times a year: Summer/Fall issue (June 15) and Winter/Spring issue (December 15). A subscription (both issues) is $15 for one year, $25 for two years, $35 for three years.

Printed on recycled paper with soy-content ink.

The Inman Chapel near Cold Mountain. (See page 41.)

Appalachia

Est. 1877   America's Longest-Running Journal of Mountaineering and Conservation

In Every Issue

Title page photo:

Navigating a thunderous chute on the Romaine River. Photo courtesy of Stewart Coffin

Front cover photo:
Blue Everest, November, 1972.
Photo by Jeffery Parrette

IN THIS ISSUE

Wonder, Never Cease

WE HIKED UP OREGON MOUNTAIN to pick blueberries in early August and came down carrying around ten pounds—when you count the antler.

It first appeared, points up like a giant claw, in a corner of my eye as I made another flailing attempt to swat away the dog-day mosquitoes. Intact, except for a tiny nibble on one outer spike, this impressive headgear had once helped a moose meet its mate—or so I hope. The round knob that had attached it to its proud owner now looked, in its retirement, like the core of a sunflower bereft of leaves. Pale scars flowed like rivulets through the rough, earth-toned outer surface, while the underside, almost completely white, was smoother to the touch, like the inside of a thick quahog shell. Later I would puzzle over the when, how, and why, but the first thing I did when I recognized the antler was whoop with delight.

Our teenaged niece and nephew were with my husband and me on that blueberry-gathering mission. Rebekah and P.J. had been good sports during the two and a half hot miles from the back door to the high bushes, despite the heavy humidity and the voracious mosquitoes. But most of the bend, pick, plop, bend, pick, plop that had been slowly filling containers with blue bounty was being done by the two task-bound adults. The kids were mainly picking what they could eat and losing their half-hearted struggle with summer's torpor. The antler changed all that. As we leaned in to study our amazing discovery, the mood turned gleeful. Suddenly, it was a rare day.

Once it was safely down the mountain, our antler stayed at the center of everyone's attention. At first, we thought it must have been shed very recently. Otherwise, we reasoned, the mountain's rodents would have helped themselves to more than just one tiny serving of this mineral-rich delicacy. But research on the Internet (a marvel of an entirely different sort) gave us pause. The bull moose, we discovered, grows its antlers during the early summer months. The bony racks are made of phosphorous and calcium and nurtured with blood vessels contained in a brown "velvet" skin that coats them until they are fully developed. During mating season in early fall, the bull will use his antlers to warn off—or more rarely, fight off—other males interested in the same female. Once the moose has won his prize, he sheds his antlers and begins storing up the minerals that will allow him to grow an even larger rack the following year.

How was it possible, then, for us to find a nearly untouched antler in the woods in August? When we posed this question to wildlife biologist and Fairbanks resident Jeff Fair (a.k.a. Yukon Jeff), one of *Appalachia's* editors at large, he had a ready answer. So did our friend John Drew, a biology teacher at Concord Academy, and wildlife biologist John Lanier of New Hampshire, who has observed moose behavior closely. They all agreed that the moose had to have shed this antler the previous winter. In August, antlers are just reaching full development, and if for some reason this one had been shed that month, it would have been covered by at least some of its velvet.

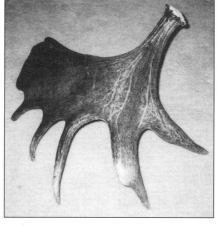

Photo by Susan Stott

What remains intriguing is why the antler had not been devoured. Maybe it had landed in a tree and stayed there until just before I spotted it; maybe the moose had shed it quite late, after the worst of the winter hunger had passed. We'll never know. And that is what I love best about this antler. It infused a groggy day with energy, it piqued the curiosity of everyone who saw it, it prompted quick response from three busy biologists, and it helped me remember that you don't have to live on the edge to experience a breathtaking moment. But most of all, it kept part of its natural mystery to itself. Small wonder it still brings me such delight.

—Lucille Stott
Editor-in-Chief

A New Look for *Appalachia*

This year Appalachia turns 128. Since the AMC's founding in 1876, its companion journal has provided members with information, insight, and inspiration about the nearby White Mountains and all "adjacent regions." Much has been written about the vision of the scientists and explorers who founded the club and inaugurated this journal, but less widely known is the long view they took of "adjacent regions." When E. C. Pickering wrote in 1877 that "adjacent" should include the Himalayas and "even the lunar mountains," he set the club—and its journal—on a path of boundless exploration.

With this issue, Appalachia is following AMC tradition by embarking on an adventure that will take it to some hitherto unexplored adjacent regions. Besides being available, as always, to members of the AMC, the journal will also be distributed more widely in select bookshops. To correspond with this wider distribution, the journal has undergone a modest style makeover—one that we believe honors the publication's history while refreshing the look of its pages. The familiar elements that appear in every issue—Accidents, Alpina, Mountain News and Notes, poetry, and nature photography—have all been maintained. The only difference is the more up-to-date look, including crisper, cleaner fonts and a more consistent cover banner. See what you think. We will be interested to know your reaction.

Over the years, many AMC members have asked for clarification about how to subscribe to the journal so they will be assured of receiving both issues of Appalachia each year. If you are not already a subscriber, here is what you can do:

- Check the Appalachia subscription box on your AMC club membership form when you renew your membership each year. You are given three choices:

    3-year subscription for $35
    2-year subscription for $25
    1-year subscription for $15

- Fill out and mail the subscription form at the back of this journal.
- Subscribe online at www.outdoors.org.
- Call 800-262-4455.

If you currently receive the journal, a renewal notice will appear only once, in your last issue. Remember, gift subscriptions are available for your family and friends!

We hope you enjoy Appalachia's new look and that you will spread the word about our journal to all of your friends and neighbors. We appreciate your support and look forward to many more years of discovering adjacent regions with you.

—Lucille Stott
Editor-in-Chief
stottdan@rcn.com

High on Lhotse Face just below South Col during the successful 1991 New England Everest Expedition led by Rick Wilcox, which placed four out of eight members on the summit in a very challenging season.

Opposite page: *East Face of Everest from Makalu.* Photo by Rick Wilcox

Fifty Years of Climbing Everest

1953–2003

Jeffery Parrette

The First Ascent[1]

On the morning of May 29, 1953, two men struggled up a steep, unstable snow slope on the Southeast Ridge of Mount Everest.[2] The taller of the two was a 33-year-old New Zealander, and the other was a 39-year-old Sherpa. They were dressed in thick down clothing covered by windproof suits, and they wore massive boots, gaitered and cramponed. Their faces were hidden by dark goggles and the masks of their oxygen sets. The faces behind the masks were stiff and tense; they thought this was one of the most dangerous places they had ever climbed. There could be no thought of turning back—they fully intended to climb Everest and were about to pass the South Summit and climb higher than man had ever done.

The night before, Edmund Hillary and Tenzing Norgay had eaten well, forced down quantities of lemon drink, and slept fitfully on limited quantities of oxygen in the tiny, unevenly floored tent that was Camp IX, the highest camp ever placed. There was a stiff wind early in the night, but it dropped, and the morning was as good a day as one could hope for high on Everest. After sardines, biscuits, and more lemon drink, followed by a long struggle to thaw Hillary's frozen boots, they set out at 6:30 A.M. Each was carrying about thirty pounds, mostly oxygen. They moved to the right to avoid a difficult rock ridge and climbed a slope of steep, unstable snow. Pushing up the frightening 400 feet, they stepped onto the South Summit at 9:00 A.M. and rested.

Hillary then led off, and with the first bite of his axe into the firm snow, he knew it would take a lot to stop them now. Contrary to the experience of

*The rock step, later known as the Hillary Step, was deemed by Hillary to be
"a barrier beyond our feeble strength to overcome."*

earlier Everest climbers near this altitude, Hillary found, "To my surprise I was enjoying the climb as much as I had ever enjoyed a fine ridge in my own New Zealand Alps." In another hour, they reached the most feared obstacle on the ridge—a rock step some forty feet high.[3] Hillary judged it "a barrier beyond our feeble strength to overcome." But there was a crack between the rock step and the snow cornice on its east side. Belayed by Tenzing, Hillary wedged his way up, back against the rock, knee and crampons to the cornice. After a few moments rest, he brought up Tenzing. Both rested, grasping for breath, then started up again, now confident they would reach the summit.

Some of the pleasure had gone out of the climb: Hillary was tiring after two hours of cutting steps, and Tenzing was moving very slowly. Then, according to Hillary's account, "The ridge ahead, instead of still monotonously rising, now dropped sharply away, and far below I could see the North Col and the Rongbuk Glacier. I looked upward to see a narrow snow ridge running up to a snowy summit." The two climbers, still roped together, walked up the narrow ridge and stepped on the highest point of Everest, first Hillary then Tenzing.[4]

Thus was Everest climbed. The two climbers did not suffer the terrible physical weariness experienced by most of their predecessors at high altitudes on the mountain; in fact, both found part of the final ascent pleasant. Nevertheless, reaching the summit was the culmination of thirty-two years of elaborate effort. Their British Expedition of 1953 (led by John Hunt) comprised 15 members including Tenzing, 38 Sherpas, 5 Gurkha NCOs, and 350 porters. Before 1953, there had been ten major expeditions directed to the same end, eight British and two Swiss, and thirteen men had died on the mountain.[5]

At the summit, the pair rested a moment, then shook hands and embraced. They ate a bit of Kendall mint cake and performed the usual summit tasks. Hillary took what would become the world-famous photograph of Tenzing on the summit holding up his ice axe with the colors of the United Nations, Great Britain, Nepal, and India; then he shot a round of summit photos. Tenzing offered to take a picture of Hillary, but he refused. Tenzing buried a few candies, a pencil given to him by his daughter, and a small black-and-white cloth cat. Hillary buried a crucifix, and Tenzing unwound the flags from his ice axe, strung them over the summit and buried the ends of the lanyard in the snow. Both remember looking for traces of the lost climbers of 1924, George Mallory and Sandy Irvine. There were none.

After fifteen minutes on the summit, the climbers refitted their oxygen masks and, at first quickly and then more slowly as fatigue took hold, retraced the route of ascent. At Camp IX they rested briefly, then wearily pushed down toward the South Col. George Lowe met them a couple of hundred feet above the Col, and Hillary forced out, "Well, George, we knocked the bastard off." Hillary and Tenzing, too tired to respond to Lowe's enthusiastic reaction, shuffled up the short rise to the camp and collapsed into sleeping bags. They slept poorly, excited by their success and too cold, "[W]e lay there for half the night reliving all the exciting incidents and murmuring to each other between chattering teeth."

The next day Hillary and Tenzing, shepherded by Lowe and Wilfred Noyce, moved slowly down to Camp IV and were met on the way by Charles Wylie and expedition photographer Tom Stobart. Just above Camp IV, they saw other members of the expedition hurrying toward them. They plodded on, heads down, until Lowe pointed to the summit with his ice axe and gave the thumbs-up signal, whereupon the welcome exploded into a scene "rather more emotional than is expected of members of the Alpine Club, but it was a day, after all, that will never be equalled in the lives of any of us."[6]

At Camp IV, Hillary recounted the climb as *Times of London* correspondent James Morris (later the distinguished writer Jan Morris) feverishly took notes. Morris realized that, if he moved quickly, the news might reach Britain in time for the coronation of Queen Elizabeth II, so he immediately descended to Base Camp and sent a runner to the Indian radio post in Namche Bazar with a coded message, which was relayed to the *Times* in London. On the morning of coronation day, June 2, the *Times* distributed the story to the crowds gathering in the streets for the coronation procession—a fairy tale cap to the first day of what some were already calling "the second Elizabethan age." London, England, Great Britain, and then the world burst into a cloud of excitement, adulation—and politics. In the excitement, everyone was too polite to point out that Everest, the "British mountain," had been climbed by two men who were not British and who had never seen Great Britain.[7]

Certainly, Hillary and Tenzing were fortunate—in their well-organized supporting expedition, in the weather, and in their own mental and physical strength—but the world, too, was fortunate in the pair who first climbed Everest. Neither was a sophisticated man; yet, when subjected to the fantastic pressures of publicity and politics following the climb, they reacted with wisdom and dignity. For many people of the East, Tenzing became a symbol of emancipation from colonial power; however, he resisted those who wished to manipulate him for their own ends. Despite all the slights and misunderstandings that might have driven them apart,[8] Hillary and Tenzing always showed deep regard for each other. Both used their fame to benefit the Sherpa people. Though they remained adventurers and mountaineers for many years, they understood the peril of anticlimax: neither ever climbed on Everest again.

For some British mountaineers, the ascent of Everest was a deliverance. Everest had to be climbed right enough, but the efforts required were too elaborate, too reminiscent of military campaigns, too *professional*, to fit the amateur image of British mountaineering. It was perhaps with this in mind that John Hunt wrote in his diary on the night of May 30, 1953, "Thus ends the Epic of Everest." He was quite wrong.[9]

National Expeditions

Hunt may have been a poor prophet, but his success as an expedition leader established the model used by Everest expeditions for years. It was no longer argued that a small, fast-moving group might have a better chance of success. Massive preparation and the generous use of supplemental oxygen had worked; huge, costly teams of climbers, Sherpas, and porters were thus necessary. Until 1971, this perceived requirement and the need for diplomatic negotiations to gain permission limited Everest efforts to official or quasi-official major national expeditions.

The French were scheduled for a 1954 expedition but decided to abandon their reservation in Gallic contempt for a mere follow-on to the British first ascent. The less sensitive Swiss made an attempt in 1956. There may indeed have been some disinclination to be merely number two; only one veteran of the 1952 Swiss expeditions joined Albert Eggler's 1956 attempt. When his lead team reached the South Col, Eggler courageously ordered the men to turn their backs on Everest and attempt Lhotse; Ernst Reiss, the holdover from 1952, and Fritz Luchsinger made the first ascent of Lhotse on May 18, 1956.

View of Everest and Lhotse from the Western Cwm.

Jürg Marmet and Ernst Schmied became the second pair to ascend Everest on May 23, and two more Swiss reached the top the following day.[10]

Indian Premier Pandit Nehru met Tenzing after his climb of Everest and decided to found the Himalayan Mountaineering Institute in Darjeeling with Tenzing as "Chief Instructor." By 1960, the Indians were ready to try Everest. The expedition of 23 members and 800 porters was led by Brigadier Gyan Singh; the climbing team was trained and largely selected by Tenzing. On May 25, the Indians reached the South Col and, in bad weather, the foot of the South Summit at 28,300, but then retreated. One of the three who reached 28,300 feet was a Darjeeling Sherpa named Nawang Gombu, who was to be heard from again.[11]

Also in 1960, the Chinese claimed the first ascent by the Northern Route—a profound shock to Western mountaineers, who did not consider the Chinese to be climbers. In fact, in 1955 the Chinese government, assisted by Soviet Russia, had begun a major program of mountaineering development. Led or helped by Russians, the Chinese ascended several high mountains in China and Tibet, including the first ascent of Mustagh Ata (7,456 m). In 1959, with three Russian climbers, they made a mountaineering reconnaissance of

Everest, which did not reach the North Col. A joint Sino-Russian effort was planned for 1960, but by then their Socialist brotherhood had deteriorated, and the Russians were no longer welcome.

The Chinese accounts of the claimed victory were long and rambling, with frequent lapses in time sequence and improbable assertions larded with the cant then typical of publications from Communist countries. In particular, the explanation of the surprising success was not calculated to appeal to Western mountaineering thought. The victory was attributed to:

> The leadership of the Communist Party and the unrivalled superiority of the socialist system of our country. . . . the fact that we had followed the strategic thinking of Mao Tze-Tung, that is to scorn difficulties strategically, while paying full attention to them tactically . . . [and] . . . the fidelity of our mountaineers to the Communist Party and the people, their confidence in the victory of the revolutionary cause, their collective spirit of solidarity, friendship and brotherhood which they had displayed to the fullest extent, their noble quality and communist style of sacrificing the self for the honour of the collective.[12]

The story of the ascent itself was also a little too much for Western mountaineering pundits. On their first attempt at the Northern Route, which had been repeatedly tried unsuccessfully by the British between the wars, the Chinese had put three climbers with no more than two year's experience on the summit. The three made the last portion of the climb without oxygen, at night, and at least in part on their hands and knees. When they reached the top, they had been without food and water for nineteen hours. They then climbed back down, still without food and water for (in some accounts) another eleven hours. All this had happened while the Indians on the other side of the mountain were in a severe storm. There were no summit pictures (although the climbers said they had left "the five-star national flag, a note in a glove and a small plaster bust of Chairman Mao Tze-Tung"), and the pictures initially released did not seem to have been taken from a high point.

There was a flurry of disbelieving commentary. The British found it all very galling and generated a series of analytical articles about the photos. The British believed that the Second Step was *the* major difficulty on the "Mallory Route," and that once this obstacle was passed, reaching the summit would be relatively easy. (Later explorations by Westerners have shown that the trip to the top from the Second Step is not a simple matter.) When the Chinese released a picture that they claimed was taken above the Second Step, at 8,700 meters, and careful geometry and photographic comparison verified that elevation, the doubters grumbled but retreated in disarray.

But the Chinese again lost credibility after two wild claims in the sixties. They then announced a massive success in 1975, claiming nine summiteers, of whom one was a woman. Again the cynics expressed their doubts, but this time the Chinese had left a survey tripod that was found by British climbers on their summit ascent of the South West Face in the fall of that year. Of course, telling the truth in 1975 does not prove that one told the truth in 1960, and no one ever found the plaster bust of Mao Tse-Tung, but the 1960 Chinese ascent is now generally accepted.[13]

The American year on Everest was 1963, and the American Everest Expedition was the biggest and brassiest ever—the apotheosis of Hunt's large-expedition model.[14] This huge effort was largely the creation of one man: Norman Dyhrenfurth. He was a climber who participated in the fall 1952 Swiss expedition to Everest, and expedition organizer, a motion picture photographer, director, and producer—and a highly skilled promoter.

This last talent was vital. While America was undoubtedly a wealthy nation, in the early sixties there was no enthusiasm for expending that wealth on an Everest expedition. There was no nationwide mountaineering tradition and, after all, Everest had already been done. But National Geographic needed a striking theme for its 75th Anniversary Issue, and Dyhrenfurth persuaded the publishers to provide major support for an American expedition to Everest. He then arranged contracts from U.S. government agencies to fund various scientific endeavors on the expedition—principally "studies of mind and body performance under the stress of high mountains." This introduction of "damned science" into mountaineering expeditions was criticized by small-expedition advocates, because the additional cost of feeding and cosseting the "useless mouths" often equaled the grant money acquired. Dyhrenfurth minimized this effect by choosing primarily skilled mountaineers for his scientific team. He ended up with the most highly educated group ever to attempt the mountain, most of whom were also competent mountaineers. The resulting expedition was, nevertheless, the largest and most costly up to that point. As it left Kathmandu on February 20, 1963, it comprised 909 porters, 32 Sherpas,

20 members, and 27 tons of baggage, forming a four-mile "millipede," that took two hours to pass any point.

At the end of the second day's march on the long trail to Everest, the members met after dinner to discuss the expedition goals. The idea of a new route, the West Ridge, had surfaced, and in a burst of postprandial euphoria, this was expanded into the first traverse of the mountain, perhaps even a double traverse. Dyhrenfurth felt constrained to bring these lofty goals down to earth, pointing out that the major sponsors expected a successful climb to the summit and that no glorious failure on a harder route would be acceptable. But the West Ridge *had* become an objective. For two members, Willi Unsoeld and Tom Hornbein, the West Ridge immediately became more than an objective; it became an obsession.

The expedition established Base Camp on the Khumbu Glacier on March 21. The next day, the climbers began their exploration of the route through the Khumbu Icefall. Since they had first glimpsed it in 1921, Western mountaineers had considered the icefall a dangerous route, but it was by far the easiest way from the south. In an amazing run of good fortune, hundreds of men had—with trepidation—safely traversed the icefall since it was first entered in 1951. The Americans felt this trepidation, too, but comforted themselves with the thought of the twelve years without an accident.

All went well on the first trip into the fall, and on May 23 two teams moved up to improve the route. When a massive ice wall collapsed, the three-man leading rope was caught in the debris. Dick Pownall was dazed but unhurt; Ang Pema was dug out with lacerations and a skull fracture; and twenty-seven-year-old Jake Breitenbach, one of the few professional mountaineers among the members, was buried beneath tons of ice. There was no hope—not even of recovering his body.

The death was a major shock to the expedition. Breitenbach was the first man to die in the Khumbu Icefall, and the first Western expedition member to die on Everest since the disappearance of George Mallory and Sandy Irvine in 1924. But, to quote Hornbein:

> We still had to climb the mountain, for too many reasons—most simply and materially because there was too much invested, too much at stake for the entire expedition to turn around and return home at this point. . . . All felt the strong need, the desire, to go on, not only for Jake, but also for each of us individually and as a group.[15]

And go on they did; the first order of business—to climb Everest by the easiest route—went smoothly. At 6:15 A.M. on May 1, big Jim Whittaker and Nawang Gombu set out from Camp VI on the South Col in 60 MPH winds and temperatures of –20°F. Despite the wind, the cold, and fifty-pound packs, they reached the summit in just seven hours. Whittaker planted a large American flag on a sturdy pole at the top of the world—no puny pennants for the Americans. The ascent was the earliest and easiest in the short climbing history of the mountain.

The West Ridge, a more complex and difficult task, did not proceed smoothly. There was an oxygen shortage, a Sherpa problem, and a windstorm that destroyed a vital camp on the ridge. The final plan was audacious. Unsoeld and Hornbein were to climb from their camp on the West Ridge out onto the North Face and, via the "diagonal ditch" and the couloir later named for Hornbein, to the summit. There they would meet Lute Jerstad and Barry Bishop climbing up from the South Col to guide them down. There would be four summiteers, a new route, and the first traverse—in Dyhrenfurth's words, "a one in a thousand chance."

Delayed and disoriented by a fire in their tent on the morning of May 22, Jerstad and Bishop did not reach the summit until 3:30 P.M. They waited for 45 minutes, peering down the West Ridge, then began a slow retreat. Hornbein and Unsoeld, delayed by route-finding difficulties on the unexplored North Face, did not reach the top until 6:15 P.M. in the glow of the setting sun. They began to follow their predecessors' tracks down the South East Ridge but lost them in the gathering darkness. The teams made contact at 7:30 by shouting and were united by 9:30. No one had an operating flashlight, and they eventually had to settle down for the highest bivouac ever. After the long night with its pain and frostbite, all four moved down to the welcoming arms of Dave Dingman and Sherpa Girmi above the South Col.

And so the Americans triumphed: They had placed six on the summit—two by the first route chosen not as the easiest but as the best challenge—and they had made the first traverse. Magnificently told in Hornbein's book in the Sierra Club exhibition format, with Barry Bishop's iconic photo of Hornbein and Unsoeld approaching the West Shoulder and the accompanying Goethe couplet: "Whatever you can do, or dream you can, begin it./Boldness has genius, power, and magic in it," the story was a romantic tale of American can-do and individual effort.

This story had a tragic side. As Hornbein noted, "For them [Unsoeld and Bishop] the Expedition had ended. Now all that remained was weeks in bed, sitting, rocking in pain, waiting for toes to mummify to the time for amputation." And Jake Breitenbach was dead.

Triumph or tragedy, apotheosis or not, the American expedition was not the last of the national series. The Indians, who had failed again in 1962, succeeded in 1965, putting a total of eight climbers on the summit by the South East Ridge Route; among them was Nawang Gombu, who became the first man to climb Everest twice. In a confused series of expeditions in 1969 and 1970, the Japanese eventually climbed the South East Ridge route, losing one Japanese and eight Sherpas; the Sherpas all died in the Khumbu Icefall. The Italians succeeded by the same route in 1973, and the 1975 Chinese expedition from the north put no less than nine climbers on top, with one death.

Handicaps and the Handicappers

The Hunt model, meanwhile, had become obsolete. Among leading mountaineers and the major alpine countries, it was no longer enough to climb Everest by the easiest route. The clearest exposition of the grandiloquently named topic: "Mountaineering Ethics" was made years ago by the American mountaineer Lito Tejada-Flores.[16] To paraphrase — and greatly telescope — his thoughtful article:

> Mountaineering is a game. The rules of the game differ depending on the objective difficulty of the mountaineering effort. For climbing Everest, almost anything goes; for easy bouldering, the rules are elaborate and severe. As technique and equipment improve, the rules of the game are modified to maintain a suitable level of difficulty and risk.

In other words, Hunt's big-expedition model operated with such efficiency that one must now offer Everest a handicap to keep the game "fair."

Other than choosing a more difficult route as the Americans had done in 1963, the first handicap to be offered and overcome was "climbing while female." During the long period when a barrier seemed to exist at 28,000 feet on Everest, preventing climbers from going higher, a few theorized that women might have a physiological advantage for very high altitude climbing (perhaps an insulating subcutaneous layer of fat, ignoring the obvious point that many capable male climbers had adequate layers of fat—subcutaneous and otherwise). More typical was the attitude of Sir Francis Younghusband, a fixture on the "Everest Committee" of the 1920s and 30s, who believed that Everest was fated to be climbed by "islanders from the North Sea." Said Younghusband, "The more necessary is it, then, that *young men* with ambition for climbing should prepare themselves to gain the great prize. . . . For Everest will accept defeat from none but the fittest in body, mind, and spirit."[17] He would have been surprised to learn that, before the first "islanders from the North Sea" reached the summit of Everest in the fall of 1975,[18] two women—oriental women at that—had already been there.

In 1975, Mrs. Eiko Hisano led the Japanese Ladies' Expedition up the usual route from the south. On May 4, an avalanche from Nuptse struck Camp II in the Western Cwm injuring members Junko Tabei and Yuriko Watanabe. Nevertheless, on May 16, Mrs. Tabei and Sherpa Ang Tsering left Camp VI on the South East Ridge at 5:00 A.M. and, Ang Tsering leading all the way, reached the summit at 12:30 P.M. Tabei, the first woman to climb Everest, is sometimes described as "a Japanese housewife." Not really. She is an ex-schoolteacher, and a remarkable athlete and climber, who had previously ascended Annapurna II. Just eleven days after Tabei's summit victory, a Tibetan woman named Phantog, from the 1975 Chinese north side expedition, joined a climb from an 8,680-meter camp to the summit. Phantog was also not a housewife. She had previously ascended both Mustagh Ata and Kongur Tiube Tagh, and on Everest she was chosen to lead the "second assault rope," which included two highly skilled male climbers.

The first European woman to climb Everest, on October 16, 1978, was Wanda Rutkeiwicz of Poland.[19] The second was Hannelore Schmatz of Germany, on October 2, 1979. Schmatz died on the descent—the first female death recorded on the mountain. The first ascent by an American woman occurred nine years later: Stacy Allison reached the top on September 29, 1988.

By the end of 2002, seventy-five women had climbed Everest—six of them twice. Four women had died on the descent. Lydia Brady of New Zealand may have reached the top without supplemental oxygen in 1988; Alison Hargreaves of England certainly did so in 1995, as did American Francys Arsentiev in 1998.

In a Class By Himself

The next two handicaps offered and overcome on Everest were largely conceived and carried out by the outstanding Himalayan mountaineer of the twentieth century, Reinhold Messner of the South Tyrol. Messner has garnered enough Himalayan firsts for a dozen mountaineers, including becoming the first to climb all fourteen of the world's highest mountains. He shows a rare ability to attempt a feat at the edge of current possibility, and the even rarer ability to tell when he is about to go over that edge, at which time he divines the path to survival and follows it quickly and ruthlessly. To modify the venerable saw about pilots: There are old Himalayans and bold Himalayans, but there are no old, bold Himalayans—except Messner.

Between the two World Wars, there was much debate about the usefulness of and need for supplemental oxygen when climbing Everest. Arguably, the use of the heavy and unreliable sets then available gave no net advantage at all. This debate disappeared with the development of better sets and more effective theory and organization for the use of oxygen. Since supplemental oxygen *had* been integral to the successful climbs, it was deemed necessary, particularly among continental climbers and physiologists who held that those who went very high without oxygen were likely to suffer serious brain damage.

Messner did not believe this. In 1978, he bought places on an Austrian expedition for himself and Peter Habeler of Austria with the understanding that he and Habeler could operate independently and attempt an ascent without oxygen. The effort did not start well; on the first try, Habeler dropped out due to stomach problems, and Messner and two Sherpas were trapped by a vicious storm on the South Col for two days (with no oxygen, of course).

Habeler had second thoughts and tried to join an oxygen attempt by the other Austrians, but his countrymen did not welcome him, fearing another competitor for places on the summit team. Messner never wavered, and he and Habeler rejoined forces, returning to the South Col. On May 8, 1978, they climbed to the summit in eight hours. Habeler, still afraid of brain damage, made a panicked descent and injured his ankle in a sitting glissade; Messner was more deliberate, but he spent so much time filming with his goggles off that he became snow blind. As Messner said, "It was two invalids that returned to Camp 2, but at the same time we were immensely proud of what we had done."[20]

That the ascent had really been made without oxygen was doubted. Oddly, Sherpas expressed the strongest doubts, though they themselves are capable of excellent physiological performance at very high altitude. Over the years Sherpas had come to see the benefits of "English air" and viewed its use as one of the perquisites of high climbing. But, as with the four-minute mile, once the psychological barrier was overcome, others could follow. In the fall of

Photo by Rick Wilcox

Oxygen bottles on South Col.

1978, Hans Engl of Germany reached the summit without oxygen, and two days later Mingma Nuru, one of the loudest of the Sherpa doubters, did the same. By the end of the 2002 season, there had been 110 ascents without oxygen by 88 climbers. (Repeat ascents without oxygen, particularly by Sherpas, are now common.)

For his next "handicap," Messner decided to make a true solo ascent of Everest — not merely a passage alone to the summit from a high camp on a route prepared and stocked by a team, but a solitary climb from the base to the top on a deserted and unprepared route. Even in 1980, when he planned to make his try, such an ascent was hardly possible on the developed south side. But that year the Chinese decided to let foreign expeditions climb from Tibet. Messner arranged for an expedition to the north side in July, the peak of the monsoon season. "The only person to come with me was my friend Nena Hollguin, although we were obliged to take a liaison officer and a translator as far as Base Camp. It was, therefore, very much a mini-expedition, yet it cost far more money than anything I had undertaken before; more money than I could ever earn back from it. . . ."

Snow conditions were too dangerous in July. But in August Messner and Nena returned from hiking in West Tibet to a few days of fine weather and moved to Advanced Base at 6,500 m on the East Rongbuk Glacier. Messner made one relay with his ultra-light bivouac kit, then moved up in a single day (August 18) to the North Col and on to a bivouac at 7,800 m. Deep snow made the usual Chinese route impossible, so Messner moved out onto the North Face to a second bivouac. On August 20 he abandoned most of his equipment and reached the Norton Couloir, which he climbed:

> [I]t is not particularly steep, but is still dangerous — up to where it flattens out . . . that last section of the summit ridge seemed to go on forever. . . . I could not manage the last few metres — I crawled on my hands and knees. . . . I have never in my whole life been so tired as on the summit of Mount Everest that day. . . . For a long time I could not go down, nor did I want to. Finally, I forced myself to begin the descent . . . from the North Col to Base Camp, soft snow gave me a lot of trouble; I slid and fell more than I climbed down. . . . It was only when I reached the foot of the mountain and the ordeal was over, when I no longer had to worry about falling, or dying of exhaustion, or freezing to death, that I collapsed.[21]

A most remarkable individual performance: not only the first true solo (in the monsoon season and without supplemental oxygen) but a major new route. The essence of the event was that Messner was entirely independent once he left the glacier. No one had prepared anything for him; no one helped him; no one *could* help him. This complete independence is not now feasible on Everest.

Finding New Ways to the Top

Following the American lead on the West Ridge in 1963, many expeditions have challenged the mountain by the deliberate choice of a new and more difficult route. What constitutes a worthy new way up a mountain is determined by "mountaineering aesthetics," an even more inchoate discipline than mountaineering ethics. One mountaineer's "fine new route" is another's "minor

Everest Massif from the West-Norhwest (Cho Oyo). 1. North Ridge; 2. NE Ridge; 3. S Pillar; 4. Lho La. On the North Face: N. Norton Couloir; H. Hornbein Couloir. East Rongbuk Glacier, Kangshung Glacier and Kangshung Face behind the massif.

variation," and, of course, merely getting lost for a time does not count. The Everest massif is huge and by Alpine standards has room for hundreds of routes, but mountaineers have been slow to dignify variations with "route status." The table below summarizes the currently accepted list of fifteen routes.[22] Those unfamiliar with the topography of Everest may find it useful to study the image on page 26 in connection with the table.

Everest, The Routes

Date	Route	First Ascenders	Expedition
May 29, 1953	W Cwm, S Col, SE Ridge	E. Hillary and Tenzing	British
May 25, 1960*	N Col, N Ridge, NE Ridge	Wang Fu-Chou, Chu Yin-hua, and Konbu	Chinese
May 22, 1963	W Cwm, W Ridge, Hornbein Couloir	T. Hornbein and W. Unsoeld	U.S.
Sep 24, 1975	W Cwm, SW Face, SE Ridge	D. Haston and D. Scott	British
May 13, 1979	Khumbu Glacier, Lho La, W Ridge Direct	A. Stremfelj and N. Zaplotnik	Yugoslav
May 10, 1980	Rongbuk Glacier, Japanese Couloir, Hornbein Couloir	T. Shigehiro and T. Ozaki	Japanese
May 19, 1980	W Cwm, S Pillar, SE Ridge	J. Kukuczka and A. Czok	Polish
Aug 20, 1980	N Col, N Ridge, Norton Couloir	R. Messner	Solo
May 4, 1982	W Cwm, SW Pillar, W Ridge	E. Myslovski and V. Balyberdin	Soviet
Oct 8, 1983	Kangshung Glacier, Kangshung Face, SE Ridge	L. Reichert, K. Momb, and C. Buhler	U.S.
Oct 3, 1984	Rongbuk Glacier, Norton Couloir	T. Macartney-Snape and G. Mortimer	Australian
May 20, 1986	Rongbuk Glacier, W Ridge, Hornbein Couloir	S. Wood and D. Congdon	Canadian
May 12, 1988	Kangshung Face, S Col, SE Ridge	S. Venables	U.S./British
May 11, 1995	E Rongbuk Glacier, NE Ridge	K. Furuno, S. Imoto, and 4 Sherpas	Japanese
May 20, 1996	E Rongbuk Glacier, Zakharov Couloir, N Ridge, NE Ridge	V. Kohanov, G. Semikolenov, and P. Kuznetsov	Russian

* Ascent questioned. The Chinese certainly climbed the route in 1975.

Much is hidden in the table: the long international and national expedition struggle on the South West Face, called the "Hardest Way up Everest"; the British-American alpine-style epic from the Kangshung Glacier to the South Col and the summit in 1988; and the real "Hardest Way up Everest," the ascent of the North East Ridge. For that ridge, the Japanese ascent in 1995 was an anticlimax. The climax came on May 17, 1983, when the tiny figures of Peter Boardman and Joe Tasker, great mountaineers and great mountaineering writers, disappeared from sight between the First and Second Pinnacles on the ridge. The stories of the routes are the great stories of Everest and have been well told by the participants.[23]

Fifteen Minutes of Fame

In 1968, the artist and "personality" Andy Warhol said, with remarkable pre-science about the recently established era of mass communication, "In the future, everyone will be world famous for fifteen minutes." Climbing Everest to the top has been done by more than 1,000 people. If fame is to consist of more than a moment of attention at a cocktail party, there are two require-ments: Someone must record one's ascent; and one must establish primacy — quick now, who were the second pair to climb Everest? —there must be a distinction from all previous ascents.

The recording of Everest climbs has changed. Early ascents were described by expedition leaders and participants and published or summa-rized in the conventional mountaineering journals. But when the number of ascents exploded, the record keeping was taken over by those who might be called the "counters" or the "statisticians" of the Himalaya.[24] The distinctions needed to establish primacy are typically stated as: "The first [national, gen-der, ethnic or other category] to [take actions including reaching the summit of Everest, under various conditions]." This formulation has proved extremely elastic and is capable of providing whole sets of distinctions on a single theme.

For example:

> In 1979 Gerhard and Hannelore Schmatz became the first married couple to reach the summit of Everest, but they got to the top a day apart, and Hannelore died on the way down (thus achieving more permanent distinction as the first woman to die on Everest). This permitted Andrej and Marja Stremfelj to become the first married couple to reach the summit of Everest together and survive in 1990. But they used supplementary oxygen, so in 1998 Francys and Sergei Arsentiev became the first married couple to reach the summit of Everest together without the use of supplemental oxygen. But they died on the descent, so the category "First married couple to climb Everest together without supplemental oxygen and survive" remains open.

With a little ingenuity, such a series of distinctions can be extended indefinitely.

One fertile source of distinction is nationality. By the end of 2003, representatives (frequently self-appointed) of sixty-three established nations have reached the summit, and this does not count "nationalities" like the large and distinguished group of mountaineering Basques or the much smaller and less distinguished group of Jersey Islanders. Obviously, this series can be subdivided by gender. Another category is age. When Tenzing reached the summit in 1953 at age 39, he automatically became the first Old Man of Everest. But not much attention was paid to the age of Everest climbers until American Dick Bass reached the top in 1985 at 55. The category has suffered from squabbling over the exact age (number of days beyond one's birthday) and just how much aid an oldster should receive from his comrades, but the current Old Man, Yuichiro Miura, reached the top at 70 years and 222 days in 2003. He should hold the title for a while. The current Old Woman is Tamae Watanabe, who was 63 when she reached the top in 2002.

Interest in "Fast Ascents" began with a remarkable alpine-style climb of the North Face by Swiss Erhard Loretan and Jean Troillet. On August 28, 1986, they skied across the Rongbuk Glacier to the foot of the face and started up at 11:00 P.M. Pressing on that night and the following day and night, they reached the summit at 2:00 P.M. on August 30—39 hours later. They spent an hour on top, then returned to the base of the face in just 3 1/2 hours by sitting glissade, called by an envious Polish mountaineer, "the world's greatest arse slide." The round-trip took just 43 ½ hours, at the time a revolutionary event. The Fast Ascent category is now dominated by Sherpas; the 2003 record holder is Lhakpa Gelu Sherpa, who climbed the South Col route in just 10 hours, 56 minutes and 48 seconds. His total time, up and down, was 18 hours, 20 minutes.

The arse slide is not, in fact, the fastest way down Everest. The mountain has been descended by ski, snowboard, and paraglider. The first ski descent, though it was not from the summit, was made in 1970 by the current Old Man of Everest, Yuichiro Miura, then 37. The fastest descent method so far is the paraglider; Claire Berner-Roche and Bertrand Roche lugged a tandem paraglider to the summit in 2001 and flew down from 100 meters below the top to the north-side Advance Base Camp in just eight minutes.

Another category contradicts Younghusband's pronouncement that "Everest will accept defeat from none but the fittest in body, mind, and spirit." With the improvement of routes and the broader access granted by commercial expeditions, climbers with physical handicaps now attempt and sometime succeed on Everest. (It could, of course, be argued that fitness of mind was never a requirement and may not even be an advantage.) Norman Croucher is a skilled climber who has two artificial legs and moves uphill on crutches. In the 1993 post-monsoon season, he reached 7,600 meters on the North Ridge, nearly 600 meters above the North Col. (This was his high point on Everest. But in 1995, Croucher, accompanied by only one Sherpa, reached the summit of an 8,000-meter peak, Cho Oyo.) Tom Whittaker has only one leg and climbs with a prosthesis that includes a built-in crampon. On May 27, 1998, he made the first ascent of Everest by a leg amputee. On May 25, 2001, Erik Weihenmayer, blind since age thirteen, followed the sound of bells on his partner's rucksack to reach the summit "in very creditable time." Weihenmayer had previously climbed McKinley and Aconcagua. These accomplishments represent remarkable adaptation and extraordinary athleticism. Think for a moment what it would be like to swing a heavy prosthesis or your entire body on crutches up a steep slope, hour after hour, in the thin air of Everest or to stumble up a rough slope, unseeing, with only the tug of a rope and the tinkle of a bell as guides. These climbs are also demonstrations of remarkable bravery. Both the handicapped climber and those who help him know that some physical failure in his struggle or a sudden storm could put all in mortal danger.

The Dead on Everest

On June 12, 1924, T. H. Somervell, one of the companions of George Mallory and Sandy Irvine, who both died on that year's British expedition, wrote in his diary, "It is terrible. But there are few better deaths than to die in high endeavour, and Everest is the finest cenotaph in the world to a couple of the best of men."[25] This is typical of the beautiful phrases written when mountaineers die and their friends wish to honor them and assuage their own grief. But cenotaph "a tomb or a monument erected in honor of a person or group of persons whose remains are elsewhere" is inapt for Everest, and the truth is less beautiful.

High on any of the great Himalayan mountains, the death or serious disability of a mountaineer immediately creates a burden too heavy to be moved any great distance by the resources that can reasonably be brought to bear. As of the end of 2002, 175 people have died on Everest; most of the bodies are still there. The same limitations and stresses that prevent the recovery of the dead make burial impractical, and the best that can be done is to pile on a few rocks to discourage the goraks—the ravens of the Himalaya—or to push the body into a crevasse. Aside from the effects of goraks, the high, cold, and dry conditions preserve the dead extraordinarily well. When Mallory's body was found on Everest, the finders remarked on the "marble-like" or "alabaster" appearance of his exposed mummified flesh—after seventy-five years. Many of the dead lie at or near the place of their death, often in full view from the major routes, enduring but ineffective warnings to their successors.[26]

And who are the dead? Almost half of them (44.6 percent) come from Nepal and India and are usually Sherpas and porters. Japan and the UK are next with 7.4 percent each. The U.S. is further down the list with only 4 percent of the fatalities.[27]

Their reasons for climbing Everest vary: the Sherpas and porters were trying to make a living; a few of the others may have been on a "high endeavor," some were seeking their "fifteen minutes," and still others were

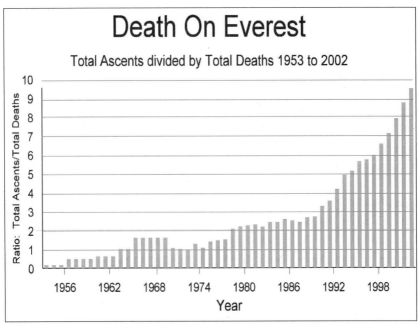

Death On Everest

Total Ascents divided by Total Deaths 1953 to 2002

As shown by the incresing ratio of successful ascents to deaths, Everest is becoming a safer place to climb.

looking for something in themselves. We can confidently assert that few thought they would die.

How likely is death on Everest? If we look at the 8,000-meter peaks, the conventional list of the fourteen highest mountains in the world, Everest has the most deaths, but that is primarily because more people climb on it than on the others. From a study covering deaths on all the 8,000-meter peaks up to 1999, and based on the ratio of total summit climbs to total deaths on the mountain, we can conclude that Everest ranks about halfway down the list, the seventh most dangerous, with a ratio of 7:1 in 1999.[28]

The risk of death on Everest *has* decreased with time. Using the same ratio of total ascents to total deaths, we can plot the diagram shown above from 1953 to the end of 2002 and see that the ratio oscillated between one and two and one-half between the mid-1960s and 1988, then began a steady and rapid improvement that continues to the present. This improvement coincides with a sharp increase in the yearly number of ascents, largely brought about by the development of the commercial expedition that offers access to all (even the marginally competent) who are willing to pay rather than just those deemed useful to the expedition.

There is a seeming paradox here: an influx of climbers, on average less competent than their predecessors, corresponding to a sharp improvement in safety. But most of this influx is not climbing in the same way. Commercial expeditions usually take the easiest way, the "yak routes" from the north and south, and provide guides—skilled Sherpas and Westerners. The yak routes are well prepared and maintained, and along them there are tents and stocks of oxygen, which can shelter and succor a failing mountaineer.[29]

The ratio of total ascents to total deaths on Everest reached about 9:5 at the end of 2002. Now, it is not clear that a rational mountaineer should consider as fair a game that results in one death for every ten successes. But the safety of this game is improving each year, and ordinary rationality does not apply to Everest. George Leigh Mallory was quite wrong in his offhand assertion that one climbs Everest because it is there. All mountains are "there"; one climbs Everest because it is the highest.

The Commemoration

In the 2003 pre-monsoon season, mountaineers flocked to the mountain in droves to commemorate the fiftieth anniversary of the first ascent. There were about 70 expeditions, all but two on the usual North and South Col routes. Stormy weather and high winds delayed serious summit attempts until the third week of May, but between May 20 and May 31 a total of 266 people reached the summit—103 on May 22 alone. (It took almost 36 years, from May 29, 1953 to May 10, 1989, for the first 266 ascents of Everest.) Only three climbers died on the mountain—a ratio of successes to deaths of 89; the overall ratio will improve sharply again. In numbers, the greatest season yet.

The mountaineering accomplishments were less great. No new major routes were established, and there were only the typical minor firsts: A seventy-year-old man took the Old Man of Everest title, and Jess Rosskelly became the youngest American to climb the mountain (greatly upstaged by Sherpani Ming Kipa, who reached the top at 15 years and 18 days of age—the youngest person ever and, by 4 years, the youngest woman); another American became the first one-armed climber to reach the summit; Appa Sherpa climbed the mountain again—for the thirteenth time; the Chinese broadcast live from the summit, not really a first—even for them; Sherpa Lhakpa Gelu climbed from the south-side Base Camp to the summit in 10 hours, 56 minutes and (it is said) 46 seconds; and Oscar Cadiach became the first Spaniard to reach the summit without supplemental oxygen.

The festival on the mountain was a rare bit of encouragement for the tourist authorities in Nepal and Tibet in an otherwise dismal season weighed down by general fears of terrorism and (in Nepal) the threat of Maoist insurgency.

Of course, the commemorative ceremonies were not limited to climbing. There were the expected dinners and speeches worldwide, but particularly in New Zealand, Great Britain and Nepal. The surviving symbol of the first ascent, Sir Edmund Hillary (Tenzing died in 1986), appeared at a surprising number of the commemorations. Now eighty-four, the towering climber of 1953 moved slowly, sometimes leaning on a cane, but despite age and years of training as ambassador of his country to India, Nepal, and Bangladesh, the bluntness of the man who announced the first ascent with "we knocked the bastard off" came through. A sampling of Hillary quotes about present-day Everest may be quite the best souvenir of the commemorative season:

On the crowds: "There are far to many expeditions at Mount Everest. I have suggested that the number of expeditions be restricted to one or two a year, but the temptation of foreign money was too great."

On fixed rope and ladders: "We had no fixed ropes or ladders, we had to do it all ourselves." In Hillary's view they have "nothing to do with mountaineering."

On repeat ascents: "After the climb, Tenzing and I both agreed and decided neither of us would return and climb it again. Why should anyone do it again? It is all gimmick now. It is not mountaineering."

On the present-day Base Camp: "At Base Camp there are 1,000 people and 500 tents, there are places for food, places for drinks, and comforts that perhaps the young like these days. . . . Just sitting around Base Camp knocking back cans of beer I don't particularly regard as mountaineering."

On commercial expeditions: Hillary is obviously not a believer in the statistical improvement in Everest safety: "The commercialized trips and the overcrowding were what caused the tragedy [in 1996, when eight died on Everest after summiting late and getting caught in an afternoon storm]. . . . You see, with so many climbers on the mountain, climbers are practically queuing up for the difficult parts. What happens then, quite a few don't get to the top till three or later in the afternoon. And then, like in this instance, the late weather comes sweeping in."

On mountaineering values: "There has been an erosion of mountaineering values. It used to be a team effort. Nowadays, it's much too everybody-for-himself. Tenzing and I got to the top together; it wasn't first one, then the other. Now it's every man for himself. Not much you can do about it. That's the way people are these days." [30]

But Hillary was avuncular when speaking of the importance of the Sherpa people and the meaning his efforts to help them held for him, and he frequently reiterated his respect and affection for his partner of fifty years before. His view has not changed from the words of his 1997 tribute, "I have never regarded myself as a hero, but Tenzing undoubtedly was."

After the Commemoration

The commemoration over, what of the future of the great mountain? If we simply extrapolate from the events of 2003, we can predict more record numbers, more expeditions, more ascents, and more deaths (but fewer deaths in proportion to the number of ascents). The mountain will be climbed a little faster and then faster still. The number of repeat ascents by one man will be pushed further, probably by a Sherpa. Still older men and women will totter or be pushed to the summit, and ingenious climbers will invent more and more distinctions of less and less importance. For the classical mountaineer, the only worthwhile change will be the invention of new routes. Fifteen routes is a laughably small number for the huge massif. There is room for perhaps hundreds more—with hundreds of new names, most showing the adolescent humor that grips mountaineers when they assign their names to their accomplishments.

On the other hand, as is often the case with human endeavors, linear extrapolation may not be an accurate predictor. The growing dissatisfaction with crowding, litter, and ecological damage may dictate a different future. The unruly Everest of today may be constrained, registered, and sanitized, becoming an enlarged and expanded version of the U.S. National Park Service's vision for McKinley.

Or, again, we must recognize that Everest can only be climbed from Tibet or Nepal and that both countries have strong exclusionary traditions. Indeed, Nepal closed the south side to climbers from 1966 to 1969, and the Chinese regime in Tibet allowed only Chinese attempts until 1980. Both countries have substantial internal unrest fostered by external organizations. They may react by excluding foreigners, or the current regimes may be replaced by other, more exclusionary forces. Access to Everest may be closed or greatly reduced for a time.

Whatever happens, climbers will still want to reach the top of Everest, and some number will succeed. And after they walk or stumble the last few steps, they will feel, at least for a time, a sense of triumph. For they will have conquered the world's highest mountain—and themselves.

Jeffery Parrette is *Appalachia's* "Alpina" editor and a regular contributor to the journal.

Rick Wilcox, who provided several of the photographs for this article, was the leader of the successful 1991 New England Expedition, during which he and three other climbers reached the summit. He owns International Mountain Equipment (IME) in North Conway, New Hampshire, and is a partner in the International Mountain Climbing School, which offers instruction in all aspects of mountain skills. He is an experienced mountain guide, who continues to lead trips to high mountains, and a popular motivational speaker.

Notes

The accounts of climbs in this article are based on contemporary writings, by participants when available. Many of these are referenced below. The best general history of the mountain is Walt Unsworth's *Everest*; the most recent edition is the third, published by Mountaineers Books in 2000. In reading contemporary accounts, one should remember the variation over time in the specification of heights on Everest. In the 1950s it was usual for publications in English, including many English translations of foreign documents, to give all heights in feet. Meters are now almost always used, except for U.S. publications. The "magic number" of 8,000 meters, the basis for the conventional list of the world's fourteen highest mountains, is the equivalent of 26,247 feet.

1. Several romantics of the British 1924 expedition clung to the notion that George Mallory and Sandy Irvine reached the summit in that year. With less excuse, later romantics have persisted in the belief. Recent discoveries (see, for example, Jochen Hemmleb et al., *Ghosts of Everest*, Mountaineers Books, 1999) and the experiences of Western climbers on the route the pair would have taken make it extremely unlikely that the belief is true.

2. The story of the first ascent has been told many times. I have based this account almost entirely on nearly contemporary accounts by the two participants: Sir Edmund Hillary, Chapter Sixteen, "The Summit," in Sir John Hunt, *The Conquest of Everest*, E. P. Dutton & Company, Inc., 1954 (Conquest); Sir Edmund Hillary, "Everest, 1953 (4) The Last Lap," *Alpine Journal (AJ)*, Vol LIX No. 288, pp 235–237; and Tenzing, *Man of Everest* as told to James Ramsey Ullman, Transworld Publishers, 1957, pp 260–278.

3. This obstacle is now known as the Hillary Step. Its apparent height and difficulty depend on the state of the surrounding snow. Oddly, Tenzing estimated it at only 15 ft. Some later climbers have made it much more; Peter Habeler guessed 25 m, about 82 ft.

4. For some time after the first ascent there was an attempt to avoid reporting who first reached the top. Indeed on June 22, 1953, Hillary and Tenzing signed and exchanged certificates stating that they reached the summit "almost together," but in his autobiography Tenzing states unequivocally that Hillary was first on the rope.

5. Three of the British expeditions were billed as reconnaissances, those of 1921, 1935, and 1951. In addition there had been three more or less quixotic attempts by single Westerners: Maurice Wilson in 1934, Earl Denman in 1947, and Klaus Becker-Larsen in 1951. None of these were true solos; all were accompanied by porters and Sherpas; Tenzing was with Denman. There was also a rumored Soviet

attempt from the north side in 1952; see Walt Unsworth, *Everest*, 2nd Edition, Cloudcap, 1989 (Unsworth). pp 345–347.

6. There was a bit of stage management here, Stobart had coached all to avoid signaling success until quite close so that he could capture the reaction on film. The scene was one of the more dramatic of the eventual expedition movie. See Tom Stobart, *Adventurer's Eye*, The Popular Book Club, 1958, pp 236–237. The quote about the scene is from John Hunt and Michael Westmacott, "Everest, 1953 (1) Narrative of the Expedition," *AJ*, Vol LIX, No. 287, p 122.

7. Hillary was, of course, a New Zealander. Tenzing was brought up to the age of 18 in Thame, a hamlet in the Solu Khumbu region of Nepal. He makes it clear in his autobiography that he was not born there but in "a place called Tsa-chu, near the great mountain Makalu, and only a day's march from Everest." Tenzing is vague about the location of Tsa-chu, but it appears that it is indeed in Tibet and that Tenzing was born there or nearby. (Ed Webster, quoted in an article in *The Observer*, Sunday, December 24, 2000.) Like many Sherpas, Tenzing lived in Darjeeling for many years, under both the British Raj and independent India. After the climb both India and Nepal claimed Tenzing as a citizen, and on his trip to England he carried both passports.

8. Most egregiously, Hillary and expedition leader John Hunt were knighted while Tenzing was awarded only the George Medal. See Amit Roy, "Coolie or knight? The palace story," *The Telegraph* (*Calcutta*), Monday, June 2, 2003. It also appears that the medals awarded to Hunt and Hillary by the King of Nepal were of lesser rank than the one given to Tenzing. In his autobiography Tenzing expressed irritation about Hillary's comments in *Conquest* on Sherpas and oxygen sets (Tenzing had probably had more experience using oxygen than Hillary) and his comparison of Tenzing collapsing at the top of the rock step to a giant fish just hauled from the sea. (In his *Alpine Journal* account, Hillary does not denigrate the Sherpas' knowledge of oxygen and applies the fish simile to himself.)

9. "Everest, 1953 (2) Sir John Hunt's Diary," *AJ*, Vol LIX, No 287, p 165. Hunt was much more prescient in *Conquest*, see p 232.

10. Ernst Schmied, "Everest 1956," *The Mountain World*, 1956/1957, Harper & Brothers, pp 157–162. Albert Eggler, "On Lhotse and Mount Everest," *AJ*, Vol LXI, No 293, pp 239–252.

11. Brigadier Gyan Singh, "Indian Mount Everest Expedition 1960," *AJ*, Vol LXVI, No 302, pp 15–27.

12. Shih Chan-Chun, "The Conquest of Mount Everest by the Chinese Mountaineering Team," *AJ*, Vol LXVI, No 302, pp 28–41, including (rather unfriendly) editorial notes by F. H. Keenlyside and (also unfriendly) notes on pictures by T. S. Blakeney.

13. In addition to the notes attached to the Chinese article in the *Alpine Journal* (all also in the *AJ*), see B. R. Goodfellow, "Chinese Everest Expedition, 1960," Vol LXVI, No 303, pp 313–315; Hugh Merrick, "Everest: The Chinese Photograph,"

Vol LXVII, No 305, pp 310–312; Hugh Merrick and L. R. Wager two notes on "Mount Everest: The Chinese Photograph," Vol LXVIII, No 306, pp 48–51. The controversy is reviewed in detail (though because of the date of writing, without knowledge of the difficulty of the route above the Second Step) in Unsworth Chapter 15, "News from the North," pp 344–359. With respect to the failure to find the plaster bust, it is also true that no one ever found any of the artifacts left by Hillary and Tenzing.

14. Norman G. Dyhrenfurth, "Six to the Summit," Barry C. Bishop, "How We Climbed Everest," Thomas F. Hornbein and William F. Unsoeld, "The First Traverse," *National Geographic*, Vol 124, No 4, pp 460–513. Norman G. Dyhrenfurth, "West Ridge to South Col, The 1963 Traverse of Mount Everest," *Appalachia* Vol XXXV, No 138, pp 1–18.

15. Thomas F. Hornbein, *Everest, The West Ridge*, The Mountaineers, 1980, p 78. First Published in 1965 by the Sierra Club and issued as Number 12 of the exhibit format series.

16. Lito Tejada-Flores, "Games Climbers Play," *AJ*, Vol LXXIII, pp 46–52 (reprinted from *Ascent*, May 1967).

17. Sir Francis Younghusband, *The Epic of Mount Everest*, Edward Arnold & Co., 1926.

18. Doug Scott of England and Dougal Haston of Scotland made the first ascent to the summit via the SW Face on September 24, 1975.

19. Rutkeiwicz was brought to Everest by the skillful promoter Karl Herrligkoffer. She later became the leading female Himalayan of the twentieth century, climbing more 8,000-meter peaks (eight before her death on Kanchenjunga in 1993) than any other woman.

20. Reinhold Messner, *All 14 Eight-Thousanders*, Cloudcap Press, 1988 (Messner) pp 73–76, and Peter Habeler, *Everest Impossible Victory*, Sphere Books Ltd., 1979.

21. Messner, pp 76–79.

22. Peter Gillman, Editor, *Everest: Eighty Years of Triumph and Tragedy*, The Mountaineers, 2000, pp 216–219. Canadian Sharon Wood's 1986 route to the West Ridge might be called a variation of the 1963 American Route and the 1996 Russian Zakharov Route could be called a new start to the usual 1960 Chinese Route.

23. See for examples: Chris Bonington, *Everest the Hard Way*, Random House, 1976; Stephen Venables, *Everest Kangshung Face*, Pan Books, 1991; and Chris Bonington and Charles Clarke, *Everest The Unclimbed Ridge*, Norton, 1984.

24. The redoubtable Elizabeth Hawley in Kathmandu, who was assisted by Michael Cheney until his death in 1988, keeps track of climbs in the Nepal Himalaya and on all sides of Everest, Xavier Eguskitza, a Basque living in England, developed and maintained a series of valuable tables. He was later joined by German Eberhard Jurgalski, and they now maintain the web site adventurestats.com.

25. T. Howard Somervell, *After Everest*, Hodder and Stoughton, 1938, p 134.

26. There have been a limited number of recoveries from high on Everest, for example the body of Pasang Lhamu, the first Nepalese woman to reach the summit, was brought down from the South Summit in1993 at great expense and difficulty. There have been proposals for mass cadaver recovery as part of a general cleaning up of the mountain, but no such expeditions have actually taken place.

27. "Everest Fatalities," adventurestats.com, posted October 24, 2002. "Everest Yearly Ascents by Nationalities (to date, 06.03.2002)," ibid, posted March 6, 2002.

28. Richard Sale and John Cleare, *Climbing the World's 14 Highest Mountains*, The Mountaineers, 2000, p 204. Using the measure "ratio of total ascents to total deaths" the most dangerous mountain was Annapurna, about 2 ascents per death. The other mountains more dangerous than Everest were Nanga Parbat, K2, Manaslu, Kanchenjunga, and Dhaulagiri. Cho Oyo, with 47.4 ascents per death was the safest of all the 8,000ers. The reference actually uses as a measure of danger the percent of summiteers dying on the descent. This makes Everest fifth most dangerous, but neglects most of the deaths on the fourteen mountains. A better measure would be the ratio of attempts to deaths, but the number of attempts, indeed even the definition of "attempt," is uncertain for Everest and the other 8,000-meter peaks.

29. Raymond Huey and Richard Salisbury, using an extensive database provided by Elizabeth Hawley and elaborate statistical methods, come to similar conclusions on the trend and the apparent paradox. See Raymond B. Huey and Richard Salisbury, "Success and Death on Mount Everest," 2003, available on the *American Alpine Journal* page at www.americanalpineclub.org.

30. Hillary's quotes are from the Associated Press, Agence France Presse, BBC and a *Life* interview.

The Real Cold Mountain in Pisgah National Forest

Danny Bernstein

Inman had pointed out to Swimmer that he had climbed Cold Mountain to its top. . . . Mountains did not get much higher than those, and Inman had seen no upper realm from their summits.

—From *Cold Mountain* **by Charles Frazier**

T HERE ARE THIRTY-EIGHT MOUNTAINS in western North Carolina higher than Cold Mountain. But thanks to Charles Frazier's bestselling novel and its recent movie adaptation, no mountain in the eastern U.S. is more famous. The novel is based on a family legend about Inman, an injured soldier in the Civil War, who walked back to his home on Cold Mountain. Ada, his love and icon, who stayed behind and tried to make a life in the mountains, is pure fiction.

The 6,030-foot Cold Mountain, located in the Pisgah National Forest in western North Carolina, lies in the middle of a triangle created by Asheville, Waynesville, and the Blue Ridge Parkway. Most people are satisfied with seeing it from the Cold Mountain Overlook on the parkway. Though its summit can be reached in a moderately difficult day hike—the trail is 5.2 miles one-way, with 2,800 feet of elevation gain—news outlets around the area talk of the climb as if it were a trek up Everest. In reality, the most difficult part of the trip is finding the trailhead within the countless back roads and dead-end coves.

The trails in the southern Appalachians are much smoother, wider, and less rocky than those in the Northeast. Though the whole area is mountainous, trails are built with switchbacks and are well maintained. Even if a trail goes straight up, hikers rarely have to use their hands to hoist themselves up. Ice

Age glaciers never came down as far as these southern Appalachians, so they are not characterized by the jumble of rocks typical of the Adirondacks and White Mountains. During the last Ice Age, the area became a refuge for plants and animals migrating from the North, resulting in a diversity of flora and fauna that occurs no place else in North America. Because of the abundant rainfall and long growing seasons, the wildflower season begins in March with bloodroot and ends in November with asters.

Even with all the *Cold Mountain* publicity, few people hike up to the summit. On an outstanding autumn Sunday, I parked opposite the National Forest Service sign just past the Daniel Boone Boy Scout Camp and found the Art Loeb Trail. Art Loeb was an ardent conservationist and a leader of the Asheville-based Carolina Mountain Club, which maintains trails along the AT. The Cold Mountain trail takes its time going up, first paralleling the road before starting to climb seriously. Three streams cut across the trail, each a good excuse to stop and wet my bandanna. As the trail takes another turn, I hear the familiar thumping of wings and see a gray-brown mass fire through the air. I have flushed out a ruffed grouse. The sudden noise always shoots through me. The bird has scared me as much as I have scared it.

Cold Mountain is in the Shining Rock Wilderness Area within the National Forest. Wilderness areas in national forests have been designated as special areas that should be left wild. In practice, this means that the area has no roads. Logging is not permitted, and only hand tools can be used to maintain the trails. Though people can camp in wilderness areas, they have to cook on stoves because wood fires are banned. Hiking groups are limited to ten people. Other rules apply, but the one that bothers me is the ban on trail markers and signs. When the Forest Service created guidelines for wilderness areas, they thought that leaving out blazes would decrease the number of hikers in the area. In reality, hikers create extra herd paths and confusion by wandering about looking for the "official" trail.

Shining Rock was one of three original areas in the eastern U.S. labeled as a wilderness. Enacted in 1964, the Wilderness Act protects "undeveloped federal land retaining its primeval character and influence." If this phrase were taken literally, it would mean woods without trails, pipe springs, or parking lot. No one would ever go there, including Forest Service employees. I prefer another clause of the Act, which describes wilderness as a place "where man himself is a visitor who does not remain." Man as a visitor is a charming

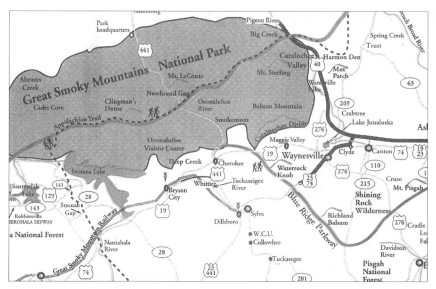

The Cold Mountain area. Printed with permission from *Adventure in the Smokies. Cold Mountain is located at the* "ni" *of* "Shining" *in Shining Rock Wilderness.*

sentiment but also a practical one. No one lives on top of Cold Mountain in the Wilderness Area. Inman's home in Black Cove is fictional.

I reached Deep Gap in three hours, having walked 3.8 miles and climbed 1,800 feet, not a speed record. There are several Deep Gaps in the area, but I assume that Inman was remembering this Gap as he enumerated the landmarks of his world: *Cold Mountain, with all its ridges and coves and watercourses. . . . Deep Gap . . .* The Cherokees arrived in this area over a thousand years ago. They called Cold Mountain *Datsunalasgunyi,* which means "Track Rock" or "Where they made tracks," because footprints were found on a rock on the mountain. By the time the novel starts, the Cherokees have been moved to Oklahoma along the Trail of Tears or confined to the Qualla Boundary, now the town of Cherokee at the edge of the Great Smoky Mountains National Park. Deep Gap was once a grassy bald where cattle grazed in the summer. Because it has not been cleared for years, hardwood trees have moved in. Several trails fan out of the Gap in different directions. An old road with many obstructions goes down the east side of Cold Mountain, into private land. The road, which I scouted on a different day, may have been the original way that wagons traveled from one side of Cold Mountain to the other.

The main navigational challenge comes after lunch: finding the Cold Mountain Trail out of Deep Gap. It is the first distinct trail to the left of the Art Loeb Trail, and I discover that it is also well maintained. Before turning on the Cold Mountain Trail, I take a digital photograph of the junction with the Art Loeb Trail. I will need to find that intersection on the way down.

The Cold Mountain Trail is steeper than the Art Loeb; I must climb more than 1,000 feet in 1.4 miles. At about the one-mile mark, I pass a couple of campsites near a piped spring. Finally, following the trail left, I reach the summit ridge. The top is still a short walk away, though with the breeze picking up, I can feel its nearness. A small, rocky outcropping, not very obvious from the trail, holds a survey marker, which tells me I am on the official summit. I share the top with three young men attending an environmental conference in Asheville. One of them, originally from Nepal and now living in Miami, entertains his colleagues with stories of the "really" high mountains near Katmandu. I hate that. Why do people praise other places while they are admiring mountains right here? I want to say, "Just look around you. Look at that view. Do you even know where you are?"

Backtracking about ten yards from the official top, I stop on an open ledge with an outstanding 180-degree panorama—and no graffiti or initials carved on the rocks. With a map, compass, and lots of patience, I identify several mountains in the distance. Straight ahead, I can see the unmistakable dazzle of Shining Rock.

When they looked back to the rocks, they saw . . . only the solid face of white rock shining in the last light of the sun. [From the novel *Cold Mountain*.]

Shining Rock, its name derived from the glittering quartz on top, is a more popular summit than Cold Mountain. One trailhead, from Graveyard Fields on the Blue Ridge Parkway, attracts weekend backpackers from all the southeastern states who may not know any other trail in Pisgah. Shining Rock, along with Cold Mountain, and 38 other peaks constitute the South Beyond 6000, forty mountains over 6,000 feet in western North Carolina and eastern Tennessee. I finished that hiking goal and received my patch in the fall of 2003.

It is difficult to know how Inman climbed Cold Mountain as a teenager before the Civil War. Before the Civilian Conservation Corps, formed in 1933, and the National Forest Service, trails were shaped haphazardly by cattle, hunters, and travelers trying to get over a mountain. After enough feet had trodden the same piece of ground, a route became a trail. We still use the word "manway" for an unofficial trail created and maintained by overuse, though I prefer the gender neutral, "herd path." Inman must have followed the most open path up the mountain. Before chestnut trees succumbed to the chestnut blight, a non-native fungus, southern Appalachian forests looked very different. Nature writings of the time describe cathedral canopies formed by chestnut trees, kings of the forest. Photographs taken in the nineteenth century show wide, clear openings between trees. Without a dense understory of rhododendron and laurels, hikers probably climbed by line of sight. They could see the top of the mountain and just headed up the best way they could. After the forests lost their chestnuts and the land was cleared by wholesale logging, other trees took over the forest, along with the impenetrable growth of heath and herbaceous plants. Bushwhacking became more difficult because there were many more bushes to whack.

Cold Mountain's story is not complete without its people, the Inmans in particular, who pepper every phone book and cemetery in the area. The real-life Inman of the novel is W. P. Inman, one of five brothers who went to war. One of the brothers who returned alive became a Universalist minister (before the church merged with the Unitarians) and built a chapel on his land. The chapel developed into a center of community activism in the early twentieth century and today functions as a venue for receptions and weddings. The present-day Inmans and others living on either side of Cold Mountain are eager to talk to city folks, partly to counter negative mountain stereotypes. They may speak slowly, but slow talking should never be confused with slow thinking.

After Cold Mountain was published, there was a flurry of activity around Pisgah National Forest to find good locations to shoot the movie adaptation. Forest rangers explained to producers that they could not film in the Wilderness Area because there were no roads going into the region. But they could get plenty of scenic shots from the Blue Ridge Parkway and on private land. Then interest ceased when Hollywood discovered Transylvania—of Dracula fame. The mountain scenes in the movie version of Cold Mountain were filmed in the Carpathian Mountains of Romania. Romanian movie extras were paid $10 a day, about a tenth of the cost of extras in the U.S. Maybe those

Photo by Danny Bernstein

A view of Cold Mountain from Frying Pan Mountain.

controlling movie budgets figured that no one really knew what the actual Cold Mountain looked like. Wrong! The novel is infused with such descriptive power that the mountain itself becomes one of the strongest characters. The real mountain is in Haywood County, North Carolina. To experience the book, you have to climb the mountain.

Seeing the mountain: Cold Mountain Overlook on the Blue Ridge Parkway, milepost 411.8.

Finding the trailhead: The trailhead starts at the Daniel Boone Boy Scout Camp. From Asheville, take I-40 West to Canton, Exit 31. Take NC-215 South through the town of Canton and continue past it; turn left on SR-1129 where there is a sign to the Camp. Stay on SR-1129 until it dead-ends into the Boy Scout camp. Once in the camp, stay to the left, past buildings, and onto the forest road. Park opposite the National Forest Service signs.

Map: Pisgah Ranger District, Pisgah National Forest, National Geographic Trails Illustrated # 780

Web sites: www.carolinamtnclub.org, www.hikertohiker.org

DANNY BERNSTEIN, a retired computer science professor, is finding and hiking all the places mentioned in the book *Cold Mountain*. She is working on a hiking/history guide to the book and can be reached at danny@hikertohiker.org.

Mountain Search and Rescue

Case Studies in Hapless Humor

Doug Mayer
Sketches by Meredith Mayer

WHEN THE PUBLIC CONJURES UP IMAGES of mountain search and rescue, the hackneyed stereotypes that seem invariably to come to mind are of grizzled veterans, bracing themselves stoically against buffeting winds as they battle their way ever upward to save the day. About all that's missing is the sword, the feisty dragon, and the poor damsel in distress.

Whom can we thank for this reliable artifice? Media eager for the sensational and a public starved for heroes both play a part. And, of course, after being depicted as heroic saviors, we rescuers don't exactly have much incentive to lay bare what is mostly a lackluster reality.

Moments of high drama do exist, of course. There is true heroism. And sacrifice does play a part: It sometimes seems as if rescues occur only at night, during bad weather, and after you've just cracked your first Guinness and settled down to a long winter dinner with friends. But the truth is, most mountain rescues are generally slow, plodding experiences occasionally punctuated with moments of confusion and, not infrequently, bouts of humor.

In the interest of editorial balance, then, it's high time to bring some of these less glorious tales to light. In doing so, I owe a debt of gratitude to my mountain friends and colleagues. Perhaps they secretly hoped that the Stokes litter-toting pal at their side would one day write of their heroic alpine endeavors. I can see the expression on their faces now, as their daydream of becoming characters in a mountaineering epic turns into something closer to a bad dream: involvement in tales of hapless mountain rescues, certain to be retold around sputtering Trangias on chilly alpine evenings for years to come.

I should also confess that I've often come perilously close to wedding a series of lousy decisions to other factors like deteriorating weather, fatigue, and darkness, nearly putting myself in need of help. My first winter hike up Mount Washington featured an absurd mix of bitter cold, cycling chaps, cotton underwear, rented crampons, and a frozen ensolite pad that shattered into slats and promptly vanished into the gathering ground blizzard. I was outfitted for a late-fall cycling tour, not the Auto Road's homestretch in January. A cascading series of unfortunate events can happen to anyone. The best we can do is stack the odds in our favor and never forget that the distance between carrying the litter and being in it is a whole lot shorter than any of us would care to believe.

The case studies I'm using here involve rescues that took place in the area around Randolph, New Hampshire. This is not because the region has some Bermuda Triangle–like propensity for backcountry absurdity, but because it happens to be my home. For better or worse, such moments happen not infrequently and in *all* locales.

To protect the rescuers, the rescued, the writer, and the writer's insurance underwriters, the names, locations, and plenty of other identifying facts have been cheerfully changed or just plain omitted.

Case Study #1: The Not-So-Very-Sprained Ankle

Background: A caretaker at a remote shelter came upon an injured hiker, complaining of a sprained ankle. After evaluation, appropriate wrapping, and experimenting with partial weight-bearing movements, the victim still insisted he was unable to hobble down the trail, even with assistance. Nearly thirty volunteers helped in the litter carry, which extended well into the evening and required several belays over steep sections of trail. It was not an easy rescue.

Outcome: The patient arrived at the trailhead, got out of the litter, and walked to the waiting ambulance. Rescuers restrained each other, then gathered at nearby homes to participate in group primal-scream therapy. Fifteen years later, they still grumble about it.

Analysis: If you weren't injured before, getting up in front of your rescuers and walking away from a five-hour carry-out in the Presidentials might assure you of an immediate injury. To avoid incurring such physical trauma, be sure to stay in the litter until you're safely in the hands of the radiologist and rescuers have consumed at least one beer each.

Case Study #2: The Vehicular Bivouac

Background: On Mount Madison in early spring, two hikers got separated. One member of the party hiked down and reported the other overdue. Fish and Game requested that the AMC check to see if their truck was still in the Pinkham Notch parking lot. It was. The next morning, rescuers gathered at the Mount Washington Auto Road for what was expected to be a lengthy search in the Northern Presidentials. On a hunch, a Fish and Game officer decided to check the vehicle again. When he did, he found the missing person soundly asleep in the back.

Outcome: The missing hiker had come down during the evening. Not seeing his partner, he opted to catch some shut-eye in the back of the truck.

Analysis: Before you start a rescue, don't just look at the vehicle. Look inside it, too!

Case Study #3: Forced Bivouac with Fully Charged Cell Phone

Background: After miscalculating the length of their hike and lacking headlamps, two winter hikers are forced to spend a frigid night out in the Northern Presidentials. The duo apparently became bored with each other's company during the night and, seeking reassurance, made phone call after phone call—several to volunteer members of the local Androscoggin Valley Search and Rescue, whose phone numbers they had tracked down.

Outcome: Come dawn's first light, the benighted hikers walked into one of the Randolph Mountain Club's cabins. The not-to-be rescuers spent a sleep-deprived, groggy day at their jobs.

Analysis: You can greatly assist potential rescuers by allowing them to get a good night's sleep before they come to look for you. Better still, if you plan on winter hiking in the White Mountains, bring headlamps, extra batteries, snowshoes, a compass, and a map—and use them before you jump right to that phone in your pack.

Case Study #4: The Case of the Sedentary Retriever

Background: New Hampshire's Fish and Game Department received a cellphone call from a hiker needing help with an exhausted dog who wouldn't budge. They were deep within a ravine in the Northern Presidentials. The only catch? Fish and Game is only empowered to rescue fellow humans. The call ended abruptly when Fish and Game admitted they weren't really in a position to rescue pets. A few minutes later, another call came in from the same hiker. Actually, what he had really meant to say was that he had misplaced the last cairn and couldn't find the trail.

Outcome: Local volunteers from Androscoggin Valley Search and Rescue trekked in that night with food for both man and beast. After a night's rest, the master and canine companion team tried again to hike out, but to no avail. More phone calls ensued. The sedentary beast was evacuated by sympathetic volunteers using one half of a two-part litter. For several Christmases later, the dog in question redeemed himself in fine style by sending rescuers gifts of fruit.

Analysis: Putting the best possible spin on your quandary shows ingenuity but is generally frowned upon. Forgo the effort, and your rescuers will be friendlier on what can be a long trip out.

Case Study #5: Mountain Misleadership

Background: At a remote shelter, a participant in a backcountry leadership class fell and injured his back. The class leader seized the "teachable moment"... and called on the omnipresent cell phone. The next morning, the group called again and insisted on a rescue. A few hours later, while several dozen rescuers were on the way in, some of the participants and one of
the leaders decided they had had enough and opted to hike out, leaving the injured person and a few others behind. They were met on the trail by a Fish and Game Conservation Officer who was, naturally, on his way in to help. In what was euphemistically referred to as "no uncertain language," the Fish and Game officer turned these hikers back up the trail to assist in the rescue of their group member. Later that morning, another volunteer couldn't resist pointing out to the Fish and Game officer that at the time of his stern lecture, he was wearing a T-shirt with a cartoon of a badge-toting moose.

Outcome: More than twenty volunteer rescuers hiked to the shelter and evacuated the patient via litter. The patient was suffering from a strained back and walked out of the hospital.

Analysis: Accidents happen, even during classes. When they do, wouldn't that be a fine opportunity to show how to self-rescue or, at least, how to coordinate a rescue? No? Okay, but if you chose to leave your injured companion behind in the woods, always remember to use a different trail from the one taken by the Conservation Officer who's hiking in to lend a hand instead of spending the weekend at home with his family.

Case Study #6: The Melted Boot

Background: On a lengthy and difficult multiday winter rescue, three rescuers were forced into a bivouac in Oakes Gulf. Later that night, the trio was awakened from slumber by the vision of a Scarpa Inverno plastic boot (later nicknamed "The Inferno") in full conflagration. The heat from the fire had melted the snow shelf the boots were on and the rest, along with a fair quantity of plastic, lace, and foam, was history.

Outcome: Later that morning, a fourth rescuer hiked a size 10 1/2 boot in to the party. Meanwhile, the ill-shod rescuer had hiked two miles on a temporary boot cut from an enso-lite pad. (To this day, he receives comments from friends asking if his boots are warm enough.)

Analysis: Gravity, when combined with superheated snow from a nearby fire, can have disastrous results on burnable footwear. Tip: when using the interagency Mount Washington repeater to call for an extra boot, try to couch your language in overly technical, obfuscating terminology to avoid having fifty rescuers eject their morning coffee through their noses.

Case Study #7: A Relationship Not Worth Rescuing

Background: Many years ago at Pinkham Notch, a call came in from Massachusetts reporting that a friend was overdue. His car was located in the Pinkham parking lot. Searchers fanned out and started combing the trails. Rescuers started to become puz-zled, however, when no tracks were found on area trails. Two days later, a hiker walked into the Pinkham Notch center and announced, "I think you've been looking for me?" He was bone dry.

Outcome: After some probing into the "hiker's" tale, it was ascertained that the man had falsified his own disappearance so that he could spend time with a woman, a fact he wanted to keep—far away—from his girlfriend. One can only imagine the final outcome.

Analysis: If at all possible, it is a good idea to keep the complexities of your personal life and the lives of volunteer rescuers well separated.

Case Study #8: Calling All Pirates

Background: Near the summit of Indian Head, south of Franconia Notch, a hiker lost his companion, who opted to fly down the cliff face and into a tree.

You might too—if you were a parrot.

Refusing to return to his more familiar perch, Pete the parrot watched as his companion dialed 911 and then proceeded to tell officials that his "friend" Pete had fallen off the cliff and was currently in a tree.

Outcome: Two Fish and Game officers responded to the scene and were rightfully more than a little nonplussed at what was either miscommunication—or misinformation. Luckily for Pete, the conservation officers left their firearms in their cruisers. Pete eventually returned to his shoulder perch.

Analysis: Keeping your group together is important. If one member of your party is clearly bird-brained and out of his familiar habitat, it might be wise to consider leaving him or her at home.

Case Study #9: In Search of . . . a Pack

Background: Descending wild and rugged King Ravine, a hiker lost the cairns amid thick fog. Frantic, he decided the wisest course of action would be to drop his pack and run out of the woods.

Outcome: Two impoverished residents of Randolph, one of whom might have been the author at an earlier age and another of whom might have been a close friend, were offered $50 each to hike in and look for the pack—and $100 each if they found it. The pack was said to contain over $1,000 in new gear, including a tent and a sleeping bag. Much "hypothetical" discussion ensued on the walk to the ravine about the ethics of finding the gear, not acknowledging it, and returning later to reap the riches of Goretex, down, and fleece. Thankfully, the pack searchers never located the gear, and their ethics remain unblemished to this day.

Analysis: Dropping everything that might keep you warm and dry and sprinting downhill—while making good use of the adrenaline surging through your veins—is generally a poor choice.

James Thurber wrote, "Humor is my sword, and it is also my shield." Once the smiles fade, it's hard to avoid realizing that these anecdotes point to our changing relationship with wild places. We are facing, I think, a perfect storm—a set if converging elements that are threatening the freedom of the mountains. When trouble arises, we seem downright recalcitrant to take personal responsibility for our predicament. Improved communications make shirking that responsibility that much easier. When the call does come in, the responsible officials are rightfully cognizant of the litigious society in which we live, and the looming fear of "what if ..." when someone is always insisting, "can't you do something?!" Confronted with such choices, it's not hard to see how sending rescuers out is a lot easier choice than giving the hikers time to solve their own predicament. Finally, we rescuers, eager to lend a hand, are ready when asked. As a consequence, backcountry values sometimes seem to be the second victim in a rescue.

Coming soon we'll have EPIRBs, emergency position-indicating radio beacons used by sailors, which promise to be a hot commodity. They're headed for the hills and just about to arrive at your local retailer. Will they make the difference between a life lost and a life saved in the mountains at some point, somewhere? Undoubtedly. Will EPIRBS result in wild goose chases, a false sense of security on the part of hikers, a false sense of urgency on the part of rescuers, and another incremental step toward bringing our front-country values into the wild? I wouldn't be the least bit surprised.

In fact, I think I hear one going off right now.

DOUG MAYER is a past vice-president of Androscoggin Valley Search and Rescue (AVSAR) and is currently on AVSAR's Training Committee. He has worked for the Mount Washington Observatory, is trails chair of the Randolph Mountain Club and is on the board of directors of the Guy Waterman Alpine Stewardship Fund. He lives in Randolph, Hampshire. The anecdotes recounted in this story were culled from the collective memories and with the assistance of Bill Arnold, Jon Martinson , Mike Pelchat, Rebecca Oreskes, Conservation Officer Doug Gralenski, and the author.

Raritan River Wetlands

I can hear the fiddler crabs only
a second or two before seeing them—hundreds
clawing across the thick mix of silty salt and sand,
retreating into their temporary caverns
a foot or two above the wetland's brackish vein.

They scuttle between stalks of phragmites—miles
of a plant too intimidating, too greedy
to grant lesser vegetation space to sprout. Standing ten,
maybe twelve feet tall, thriving in this rich muck,
the phragmites make the bounded wetland
what it is: more crowded, more confident
than the muddy marshes north of Cape Cod.

The sediment-loaded tide is rising, my time limited.
The Atlantic's rhythm of high tide, low tide—
        all waves in perpetual flow,
                all flora, all fauna in check. Gradually
the fiddlers' panic dissolves in a calm, lulled rest.

Max L. Stephan

MAX L. STEPHAN currently teaches English at the Fort Belknap Indian Reservation in Hays, Montana. He has also taught English in New York State. His work has appeared in *Lyric, Cimarron Review, Louisiana Review, Potomac Review, Black Bear Review*, and others.

Denali Autumn

Bill Sherwonit

Mount McKinley looms over Wonder Lake, 1953.

Photo by Bradford Washburn (courtesy of Panopticon Gallery)

DELIGHTFUL SURPRISE. Waking from a deep sleep, I open my eyes to a transformed world: Last night's somber overcast and heavy rain showers have given way to large patches of azure sky and a rich golden light that streams through spruce and birch and cabin windows.

Not yet ready to leave my warm synthetic cocoon, I remain huddled in my sleeping bag until noises drift down from the loft. Friends are waking, stirring. Four of us, all writers of one sort or another, have come north from Anchorage to spend an autumn weekend in Denali State Park, sometimes called "Little

Denali" in deference to its larger and more charismatic federal neighbor. Pursuing a modicum of comfort in the midst of wildness, we've settled into a public-use cabin built along the shores of Byers Lake, a small liquid gem surrounded by spruce-birch woodlands.

Now sitting up, I gaze through the cabin door's glass portal and am greeted by dazzling whiteness: 20,320-foot Denali looms above lake, forest, snow-dusted foothills, and several waves of jagged Alaska Range mountains. North America's highest peak may officially be called Mount McKinley, but we Alaskans prefer the older and more appropriate Native name, which translates to "The High One." Looming more than 18,000 feet above its surrounding terrain, Denali seems the perfect symbol of Alaska, place of superlatives and extremes. Though more than 40 miles away, on this morning it appears to rise just beyond the lake's forested edge, as if we could easily hike to its base.

Outside the cabin, we gawk at Denali and cheer our good fortune: In summer and fall, the mountain is visible only one day in three. A plume of snow blows off the summit, signal of extreme winds. Even as we watch, the plume expands and metamorphoses into a huge streamlined mass of interlayered lenticular clouds, one stacked upon the other. The lenticulars gradually merge into one huge streamlined mass with a tail of more cottony cirrous that tapers to the north. It's as though some gigantic, vaporous sky being is gobbling Denali's uppermost slopes.

While we sip coffee and delight in the great peak's company, a red squirrel busily flings cones from the top of a spruce. This harvest will be crucial to its winter survival and several dozen already cover the ground. The soft thuds of cones hitting forest floor are mixed now and then with a loud CLANG, as the squirrel's random tosses occasionally strike the cabin's metal roof. Now and then the squirrel stops his cone gathering and chatters loudly. Is he too celebrating this fine morning, or warning us to stay beyond the range of his organic missiles?

Shifting my gaze from mountain to spruce, I see a strange sight: Small, white, diaphanous clouds drift from the tree top. Squirrel is hidden from view, but the sun is at just the right angle to light up the warm, moisture-rich puffs he breathes into the cool morning air. One, two, three plumes of vapor drift from the spruce and slowly dissipate, as if squirrel were sending smoke signals or mimicking Denali.

The weekend weather changes constantly: bright sun, thick drizzly overcast, heavy rain showers, rainbows and dissipating clouds, more sun, more overcast and drizzle. Autumn snow (locally called "termination dust") creeping down the nearby foothills, then melting off. It's a perfect blend for what we aim to do: write in journals, read books, share ideas, pick berries, eat berry pancakes, hike in tundra, walk in forest, listen to bird song, watch for bear, and savor the deep colors and rich smells of changing seasons.

During one circumnavigation of Byers Lake, a sudden, cold shower ends our mid-afternoon rest break and shoos us back onto the slick, mucky 4-1/2 mile trail. Of course I've neglected to bring my rain jacket and my windbreaker is already soaked. Ellen, William, and Nancy are walking at a fast pace, but not fast enough for me. I sprint for a stand of spruce and birch trees, believing they'll provide more cover than the high grass and alders we're moving through. Running ahead of the others, I think, "This is foolish. I'm still getting drenched. I could easily slip on the mud or a wettened rock, fall, and do serious damage to my body. Or I could meet a bear." We've already seen lots of bear sign on this walk, both tracks and several piles of blueberry and cranberry rich scat and other hikers have told us of recent sightings.

These thoughts are playing in my head as I round a sharp, brushy bend in the trail. Less than 15 feet away, ambling in my direction, is a big black bear. The bear is large enough to be an adult male, which I guess him to be, and is likely growing fatter by the day as he gorges himself with berries in preparation for winter's hibernatory sleep. Apparently as shocked as I, the bear gives me a brief and startled glance then quickly steps off the trail into alder and grasses. Heart pounding, I step backwards and shout a warning to the others. But the bear wants nothing to do with us and is soon gone. It's not until later, when things have calmed down, that I even think to give thanks. But I immediately slow my hurried pace.

Sunset, our last night at Byers Lake. William and Nancy are already on their way back to Anchorage; Ellen relaxes at the cabin. I'm alone on the darkening trail, returning from a deliciously happy hour of blueberry grazing, when I come to the lake's outlet bridge. Halfway across I'm stopped by a presence that demands my full attention. Not a bear this time. Not spawning salmon or wailing loons or day's last light on Denali. Rather, bugs.

A great cloud of pale, ghostly insects hovers above the lake waters where they become Byers Creek. There are far too many bodies to count, almost too many to comprehend. Millions of them, maybe billions. In my unscientific way, I group them into gnats and midges; the largest aren't much bigger than sesame seeds, the smallest are tinier than sand grains. Most swarm within inches of the water and are thickest near the grassy shallows, but some fly several feet above my head. Many swirl in wild, chaotic dances; others seem to float upon gentle air currents like drifting ice crystals or droplets of mist.

The abundance of life is staggering. How strange, that I should encounter this amazing insect explosion—by far the largest hatch that I've ever witnessed—on a crisp night in autumn, season of endings and death. How much longer will they dance? A few hours? Minutes? 'Til dawn? In fading light, I slowly pass through this galaxy of minutely tiny organisms, encircled by an unknowable universe that's at once separate from human reality, yet somehow interwoven with our own curiously wonderful world.

I leave the insect frenzy behind, knowing it to be as remarkable as anything else we four have encountered this weekend. It's something I'll take back to Anchorage and savor as we slip slowly but steadily to that time of year we humans call the dead of winter.

BILL SHERWONIT is a nature writer who lives in Anchorage, Alaska.

Long-Legs on Mt. Wachusett

A speck of spice —
cinnamon — touring the world;
a bit of the ground
risen to go and wander.

If all our senses
were at the ends of wires;
if we had this many legs
and this little mind;

if we occupied space
as this much emptiness
arced by such brittle flesh,
we would move like them

and know how this feels:
moss, rock, dry leaf, twig,
navigated leg by thin leg,
the center lifted clear.

Polly Brown

POLLY BROWN teaches at Touchstone Community School, in Grafton, Massachusetts. She is a member of the Every Other Thursday poetry workshop;
her chapbook, *Blue Heron Stone*, is available from Every Other Thursday Press.
Recent poems have appeared in *Iris: A Journal About Women* and in *Two
Rivers Review*.

The Name Game

New Hampshire Votes to Drop Clay for Reagan

Christine Woodside

L AST JUNE, THE STATE OF NEW HAMPSHIRE announced it would change the name of Mount Clay, in the Presidential Range of the White Mountains, to Mount Reagan, after former President Ronald Reagan. The name was embraced by the New Hampshire legislature on August 16, 2003, thereby removing the name of Henry Clay, an influential nineteenth-century senator and statesman, from mountaintop posterity. The last time New Hampshire changed a mountain's name was in 1913, when Mount Clinton—which had honored former New York Governor DeWitt Clinton— became Mount Pierce, after former President Franklin Pierce, a native son of New Hampshire.

This time, however, it will take several years for New Hampshire's decision to be recognized at the federal level, a necessary step before the name change becomes carved in granite. All such changes must be approved by the U.S. Board on Geographic Names, the volunteer body affiliated with the U.S. Geological Survey (USGS), and board rules forbid the commemoration of a person who has not been dead for at least five years. So, as far as the USGS is concerned, the 5,533-foot summit rising from the Presidential Range a mile north of Mount Washington, remains Mount Clay—for now.

Despite that delay, the staff of the Ronald Reagan Legacy Project considers the name change a great achievement. The organization, based in Washington, D.C., has lobbied since 1997 to name a landmark in every U.S. county after the fourtieth president. This is the Reagan project's first mountain— indeed, its first geographical landmark. Of the fifty-two successful projects thus far, fifty-one sites named for Reagan are manmade structures, roads, or enterprises. There are eighteen buildings, fourteen highways or roads, one airport, a set of commemorative stamps in Grenada, two new varieties of roses, a

Backpacker on the summit of Mt. Clay stops to view the Great Gulf Wilderness and Nothern Presidentials.

missile test site in the Marshall Islands, a professorship, and several paintings, sculptures, and markers.

Paul Prososki, the former executive director of the Ronald Reagan Legacy Project who now lobbies for an affiliated group, Americans for Tax Reform, said that even though Reagan was not from New Hampshire and did not visit the state very often, his name belongs in the Presidentials. "New Hampshire is a very conservative state," Prososki said, "and they like the rugged individual type image that Mr. Reagan portrayed. We have some very good activists in the state who led the charge there. They didn't want a street here or a road there. They wanted something big."

The move to name a mountain after Reagan began a few years ago. New Hampshire Rep. Kenneth Weyler, a Republican from Kingston in Rockingham County, said a constituent wrote to him asking why there wasn't a mountain named after Reagan. Weyler tried submitting a bill in 2002 but was too late to have it considered in that session. He then filed HB 82 on January 8, 2003. His bill originally called for renaming Boott Spur, on Mount Washington. Weyler said he reconsidered this choice after Rep. Richard T. Cooney, a Republican of Salem (a member of the subcommittee formed to consider the Mount Reagan bill) suggested choosing "a real mountain," as Weyler recalled. They chose one of the peaks of Moat Mountain. "So, you'd think, 'No problem changing the name—it doesn't mean too much, and nobody will be insulted,'" Weyler said. He added that he wasn't prepared for the reaction of Speaker of the House Gene Chandler, a Republican from Bartlett, who suggested that Moat Mountain's name was too popular.

"We looked at the Presidential Range, and most of them are named after presidents, except for Franklin and Clay," said Weyler. "And they felt that Henry Clay wasn't well enough known to be in the Presidentials." Echoing that sentiment was Grover Norquist, president of the Ronald Reagan Legacy Project. He said that in the end the Presidentials seemed the best place for a Mount Reagan.

While Mount Reagan represents a big change for New Hampshire, it has not registered on the radar screen in Washington. If the U.S. Board on Geographic Names received an application now to make Mount Reagan the official name, "It would return it," said Roger Payne, executive secretary of the board. He explained that the board, which decides on names of all physical landmarks (not buildings or roads) must follow its commemorative names policy. Until Reagan has been deceased for five years, a name change is impossible from the board's point of view.

He said the board knew about the movement to rename Mount Clay, and that it is not the board's job to stand in the way of local name changes. But he added that New Hampshire's change has created confusion. "Some people mistakenly think that because the state of New Hampshire has passed this bill—and we did have a lot of conversations with legislative officials—that it has changed," he said. "It has only changed in New Hampshire, nowhere else. It cannot be shown on federal maps and documents."

If New Hampshire residents and hikers take to the name Mount Reagan, and it becomes the better known name, the board will consider that as strong evidence for adopting it as official five years after Reagan's death. "The most important standard is local use acceptance," Payne said. "If this is what the state wants, the federal government doesn't care. All we care about is that the same name is used for the same feature."

A mountain provides a more striking memorial than a hospital or a segment of an interstate highway. But history has shown that controversy can intrude on mountain memorials even decades after names have been changed. Consider Mount McKinley, the highest point in North America. It was renamed in 1901, the very year President William McKinley was assassinated, when emotions were still running high. Then, in the mid-1970s, Alaskans voted to return to using the mountain's indigenous name, Denali. Alaskan officials applied to the Board on Geographic Names to make the reversion official. Just before the board was ready to act on Alaska's request, a senator from Ohio—McKinley's home state—introduced a bill in Congress calling for the mountain to remain Mount McKinley. The board put off a vote, Payne said, because members knew that an Act of Congress would supersede their decision, and they preferred to wait to see what Congress would do. But Congress has never acted on the bill, and the mountain has been known by two names for the past thirty years.

Payne noted that the same raw emotion that drove the name change to Mount McKinley inspired hundreds of name changes when President John F. Kennedy was assassinated in 1963. By the Ronald Reagan Legacy Project's count, there are about 600 landmarks named for Kennedy. Cape Canaveral was renamed Cape Kennedy at the request of President Lyndon B. Johnson, but Florida residents protested, according to Payne, because Canaveral had a long history in the state. The name has since reverted to the original, he said, and after that experience, the federal government adopted a policy of waiting one year after someone's death before attempting to rename places as memorial tributes. In the 1990s, the waiting period was extended to five years because the board felt more time was necessary for considered judgment, he said.

Then there is the case of Mount Rainier. Washington State residents have tried three times to change its name back to the native Tahoomah, after which the nearby city of Tacoma is named. They have yet to receive federal approval.

In Arizona, there is Squaw Peak, north of Phoenix, renamed by state officials as Piestewa Peak in April 2003. The new name honors the first female Native American soldier killed in Iraq. Name change proponents reportedly argued that the old name was offensive, and they believed the federal names board might waive the five-year waiting period for this reason. That has not happened.

And in New Hampshire, there is the continuing saga of Mount Pierce. When the former Mount Clinton got its new name, President Pierce had been dead for almost forty-four years. New Hampshire lawmakers applied that year with the Board on Geographic Names, and the board voted to make the new name standard. But in the ninety years since the mountain was redubbed Pierce, the old name, Clinton, has remained on one of the trails and on the name of a road near the mountain. Many experienced hikers still refer to "Clinton" when they talk about it, even though there is no longer a Mount Clinton on White Mountain maps. Payne said USGS files record two "variant names" for Mount Pierce: besides Mount Clinton, it was also called Bald Hill in a local gazeteer in the mid-1800s. In fact, the New Hampshire bill naming Mount Reagan has an amendment intended to clear up the Clinton/Pierce problem once an for all; it states that Mount Pierce is the official name of the mountain.

"Renaming or changing a name is discouraged, because it intends to create confusion," Payne said. "A name more likely than not has become well ensconced on maps or documents. If a name is changed, there will be some period of time, short or long, where there is a discrepancy between the conventional printed document and what is in the official USGS database." Payne noted that the names board was not surprised when New Hampshire went ahead with Mount Reagan. But he said, "It would have been nice if it hadn't happened, only because it wouldn't have created a discrepancy."

Meanwhile, New Hampshire's Rep. Weyler said he will do whatever he can to cement the name Mount Reagan in the collective mind of the hiking public. He hiked up the Jewell and Gulfside trails to the top of Mount Clay/Reagan in November to find that the sign for Mount Clay appeared to have been stolen. Even though he understands the name can't be official for several years, he intends to see if a sign can be erected with the Mount Reagan name.

"If there's something I can put up there, I shall," Weyler said. "I don't want to be accused of putting graffiti. I'll try to think of some appropriate thing to place up there that the first vandal can't take down. I do think it's appropriate."

CHRISTINE WOODSIDE, of Deep River, Connecticut, writes for newspapers   and magazines about the environment and American life. She and her husband thru-hiked the Appalachian Trail in 1987 and have two daughters.

Isabella Lake

Loons, rapids, beaver lodge,
kestrels, and light—light
rose and golden climbing
the feathers of clouds, rose
and purple entering the water
reeds, every shade of green
in the blueberry leaves—
and the sting of mosquitoes
as wind dies down with the sun,
as the loon's clamor announces
night coming on . . .

Robin Chapman

ROBIN CHAPMAN's poems have appeared or are forthcoming in *The Comstock Review, The Hudson Review,* and *OnEarth.* Her most recent collections include *The Only Everglades in the World* (Parallel Press) and *The Way In* (Tebot Bach).

AT Hikers Believe in Magic

By Roger Sheffer

EARLY JUNE, I'M DRIVING—not hiking (too seldom hiking)—ten miles east of Front Royal, Virginia, in search of the place where the Appalachian Trail crosses US-522. Chester Gap. It's still light out, and my meeting in Harpers Ferry is not scheduled until nine the next morning. I'd like to spend one good hour on the trail, do a couple of miles either north or south, and add to my meager total of 20 miles in Virginia. I'd like to hang out with the thru-hikers. But I can't find the damn trailhead. There's nothing, no visible sign, just a bunch of little dirt roads and private driveways going off in various directions. Crawling southeast on 522, I hit the downhill side of the gap and realize I've overshot the trailhead, so I turn around and drive back to town. Then I see an encampment of gypsies in caravans and tents on the left side of the highway and almost miss the two backpackers perched on the right shoulder, thumbs out. I pull over, open the trunk, try to clear my obvious non-hiking stuff out of the way (boxes of books, a printer, a guitar). I'm embarrassed by the hamburger wrappers strewn about the back seat, but these people aren't particular.

John (a.k.a. Pack Mule) and Emily (Pokey-Hontas) are Dartmouth students who hope to make it back to Hanover in time for fall classes. I drive them five or six miles to the Blue Ridge Motel, just north of town. I tell them a few stories. They tell me about Lone Wolf, a thru-hiker who scared a few people that spring. I hand them my card, with my email address (but never hear from them again). They keep thanking me. I have given them trail magic. I probably feel better about it than they do.

Afterwards, driving north out of Front Royal, why was I crying? I didn't know at the time, but I do now. I cried for my old self, the kid too scared ever to set out on foot like Pack Mule and Pokey-Hontas—except that one time in the Adirondacks during the summer of 1969. I was hiding from the draft, and

I realized now that at age twenty-two I could have hid myself on the AT that whole summer, invisible and perhaps more protected from reality. Later, in 1977, I did just 100 AT miles in Maine, but I could have kept going all the way to Georgia. Someone might have given me a ride, money, a place to stay. It really would have felt like magic. Nowadays, "trail magic" has become so common, it's almost like a gratuity that hikers have been conditioned to expect, a welfare check of sorts.

But in the following account of "trail magic," recorded three years ago in a Pennsylvania AT register, MacGruff sounds sincerely grateful:

> As I was crossing Rt. 325 a man in a white T-shirt asked me the "where-did-you-come-from" question. We began sharing our stories with each other. Then he asked me how I was doing on cash. I said, "Okay, I just have enough to get to Maine." This kind soul went to his car, came back to where I was standing, and handed me two ten-dollar bills. The support from people you meet is oh so overwhelming. Thank you, Dave.

The man in the white T-shirt is a *trail angel*. Dave. Sometimes trail angels give cash or food in exchange for a good story. This is the best kind of charity for the giver: no administrative costs, immediate gratification, but of course no tax deduction. The angel may think, *If I'd spent those twenty dollars on myself, they would have been wasted.* For the hiker, though, twenty dollars makes a difference. Even though MacGruff has enough cash to make it to Maine, what if he gets lost and has to backtrack ten miles on some side trail? In that case, the twenty bucks will turn out to be essential.

Another thru-hiker in Pennsylvania did even better in his encounter with trail angels, though he needed their help more desperately. He'd lost his pack—which had contained everything he owned.

> When I asked the locals if they had seen anything, they immediately responded. One family gave me a ride to the police station in Jonestown and ten dollars. Amazing! Then another two couples about my folks' age said they heard my story and drove to the station to ask if they could do anything for me. I was still in severe shock and had no idea what to say. They went home and came back an hour later with the following: two backpacks (boy scouts), two pairs of jeans, two pairs of socks, a few sweaters, long underwear (size small, I'm

Four AT thru-hikers were delighted to find trail magic of sodas and snack food at the base of Clingman's Dome in the Great Smoky Mountains.

Photo by Jason "Kronk" Thresher

6'5", 220 pounds. I really didn't care; I knew I would make anything fit!), jacket, hat, two flashlights with four sets of batteries in Ziplocks, four fresh apples, and an unbelievable amount of food.

The best detail is the batteries in the Ziplock bags. And the question is this: Did he give back equal value in his story? The hiker usually gives back to the trail angel in the form of intangibles. Like the respondent to a register survey in 2001 who, in answer to the question "What's the finest trail magic you've given or received?" answered:

On top of Killington in Vermont I talked with a grandfather and his grandson. The boy, about age ten, offered me his water. His eyes were wide with amazement about a thru-hike. He gave me Trail Magic in the form of water, and I gave Trail Magic in the form of a dream.

The story of that survey is itself the story of a small gesture of charity, or trail magic, on my part, which happened far from any trail. While going through a box of registers sent to me by the Potomac Appalachian Trail Club, I found an amusing pictorial narrative inscribed by a thru-hiker named Rook, who wrote his permanent address in the margin and requested that some kind angel send his page to him after the register was full, promising "goodies" in return. So I sent it off, and the goody he sent me was a photocopy of an entire register he had left in the shelter at Wilson Creek, Virginia, during the summer of 2001. Pure gold! Here are ten top answers to his question, "What's the best trail magic you have received or given":

1. A college acquaintance of my mother's (forty years ago) ran into my mom at a reunion. She now lives in Waynesboro [VA] and told my mom to have me call for hotel/restaurant suggestions. When I called several days out on the trail, she invited me to her home for two days with hot meals, a spare car, a spare bedroom and a fridge full of beer!

— Shaggy

2. I've knocked down all the spider webs for others.

— Wrong Way

3. Finest received: In Palmerton, PA, I was adopted from the PO by the Kratzer family. Brought back to their home for dinner, beer, hot tub, and bed. Taken out to breakfast, dropped off at trailhead, and given (actually forced, she threw it out the window while pulling away!) 45 dollars! Yep, they were complete strangers. Finest given: Rounds of beers at the Port Clinton Hotel until the 45 dollars ran out.

— Gander

4. In Massachusetts I injured myself, and a lady named Joan Canby helped me off the trail and to the emergency room. She didn't know me, had to be in her seventies. But she knew I was in trouble and she came to my aid.

— Village Atheist

PS — I'll leave a couple of pens here.

5. A foot rub on top of Swarts Mtn., VT, and a real conversation with a listener.

— Unsigned

6. A ride offered by a complete stranger at 4 A.M. on a frostier than expected night near Harpers Ferry (This incident was relayed by Easy Goer, a good friend who barely avoided frostbite). Easy had to walk out in the dark with his dog to avoid dying frozen and crossed paths with a guy who'd been out all night with his girl, but was glad to take Easy and dog miles opposite his way home. Refused pay, too!

— Big T

7. A family in Great Barrington that took us into their home. Fed us dinner as soon as we arrived, then left us alone with the run of the house thirty minutes later. They insisted that we take a zero there when it was raining the next day. Fed us the whole time.

— Panama Red and Peanut

8. The best trail magic occurred when my parents were hiking a few miles of the Shenandoah National Park with us and one day we parted ways so they could get back to the car. We got caught in a real nasty ice storm. My parents are great outdoors people but novice hikers so I was very worried about them. We were due to rendezvous at Waynesboro. When I saw their happy smiling faces at the hotel and learned by freak chance the owner of Rockfish Gap Outfitters gave them a ride (or rescued them) I was never so grateful to trail magic in my life.

— Sparrow

9. Betty "Nightingale" Cather brought me treats at the Black Oven Trail Center, and also her black mini-schnauzer "Magic." Good times to play with. [Sticker: Appalachian Trail Hike for Diabetes]

— Cesar and Maud

10. The Flying Pork Chop's mother took me to the doctor's in Gatlinburg and wouldn't leave me until she knew I was okay.

— Chaser

For most thru-hikers, it's their buddies—hiking partners they started out with or met along the way—who look out for them. They try to reconnect when separated, pass notes to each other, leave beers in the stream to cool, exchange directions to the best spring or the most comfortable and cheapest beds in the next town. Or thru-hikers have nonhiking partners who meet them at highway intersections and hand them the next care package: fresh socks, a six-pack of Moosehead, Preparation H.

I was a trail angel once in the Adirondacks, many years before I knew the term. I had hiked south three miles from the Blue Mountain Lake trailhead to eat my lunch at Stephens Pond lean-to. There I met a solitary end-to-ender from Barre, Vermont, who had stopped to rest. He was about halfway from Northville to Lake Placid, an eight-day hike mostly along rivers and lakeshores. I gave him a slushy—a box of fruit juice that I had taken out of the freezer that morning. On a hot and humid July afternoon, it was the perfect treat. In return, he gave me stories, about weird bear encounters and a troop of blind hikers moving south from Sacandaga, all hanging onto the same piece of yellow rope.

In southern Vermont, I pick up the trailhead near Bennington so I can extend northward the continuous line of AT miles I've completed beginning south of Dalton, Massachusetts. I meet no thru-hikers until Congdon shelter, where I sit at the table outside and eat lunch. I have a full box of Freihofers oatmeal-raisin cookies—much better than any supermarket cookie, the kind of product you'd have your mother buy and FedEx to you because you can't get them where you live most of the year. Two Leki poles are

Trail magic is a welcome sight any time of the day for tired hikers. But sometimes, animals can invade coolers, so it is wise to keep containers tightly sealed.

propped against the side of Congdon, one of them bent from a bad fall. A hiker is inside eating his lunch (noodles and fake cheese). I give him two of my cookies, and I talk with him as I copy the meager entries from the register. His trail name is Jiffy, and he tells me he started out in Georgia on March 3. He had just graduated from Rhodes College in Memphis as a history major. He tells me about a hiker in Massachusetts dressed in "office clothes," buttoned-down shirt and nice slacks (fair exchange for the cookies). I start back to my car and lie down in the tall grass at the top of Harmon Hill, skipping the view. Jiffy catches up with me.

"What town is that?" he asks.

"Bennington. You could buy just about anything there. More Freihofers cookies. A car, if you had the money."

He gazes at the horizon. "No thanks."

We hike together the next mile or so. I tell him to apply to grad school. He kicks a pebble into my boot. I let him pass me; soon, he's out of sight. After greeting a trio of southbounders I step on an unstable rock that looks solid. I pitch forward and land on my face, scraping my knees. I could use an angel with bandages and iodine. But day hikers like me don't rate. My car's only a half-mile north, anyway. I'll make it on my own. If I see any obvious thru-hikers walking into town (five miles to the nearest convenience store), I'll stop and give them a ride.

Why not end, then, with a little more trail magic?

4-25-91 Cold Springs, North Carolina
When I came out of the Winn-Dixie yesterday at noon, a woman saw me loading my pack. She offered me a ride back to the AT. She was a stitch—80 years old and full of stories!

—The Blister Sister

7-23-00 William Penn, Pennsylvania
I passed some guy today on the trail who had a daypack on. As I passed he told me to check the "mailbox." I didn't know what he was talking about. But sure enough down the trail there was a mailbox next to the Yellow Springs Village site, and inside was a register and two beers! I left one and hiked with the other all day. It is cooling now in the spring. I think I am ready for a cold one.

—Unsigned

7-2-00 Calf Mountain, Virginia

Hikers Beware! If, somewhere along the next twenty miles, you run into a thirty-something man with a pickup truck and a brown ponytail who goes by the name of "Paul"—BEWARE! He should be considered extremely generous and could attempt to corrupt and subvert hikers into accepting free beer and yellow-blazing. Tell him T. Snake said hi.

—Unsigned

ROGER SHEFFER teaches English at Minnesota State University, Mankato. He is a published fiction writer and a frequent contributor to *Appalachia*. Mr. Sheffer is currently at work on a book about the wit and whimsy he has found in registers along the Appalachian Trail, which he has been reading since 1988.

The World As It Is

No ladders, no descending angels, no voice
out of the whirlwind, no rending
of the veil, or chariot in the sky—only
water rising and falling in breathing springs
and seeping up through limestone, aquifers filling
and flowing over, russet stands of prairie grass
and dark pupils of black-eyed Susans. Only
the fixed and wandering stars: Orion rising sideways,
Jupiter traversing the southwest like a great firefly,
Venus trembling and faceted in the west—and the moon,
appearing suddenly over your shoulder, brimming
and ovoid, ripe with light, lifting slowly, deliberately,
wobbling slightly, while far below, the faithful sea
rises up and follows.

Carolyn Miller

CAROLYN MILLER has been published in *Shenandoah*, *Quarterly West*, *Southern Review*, *The Sun*, *Georgia Review*, and *Gettysburg Review*. *After Cocteau*, her first collection of poems, was published in 2002 by Sixteen Rivers Press.

The Fellowship of the Trail

Early Cooperation Among American Hiking Clubs

By Josh Greenfield

U RBAN POPULATIONS IN CITIES across the United States soared during the final decades of the nineteenth century. Among those millions of city dwellers were some who hungered for wilderness, and in Boston, San Francisco, Portland (Oregon), and Seattle, they came together to form hiking clubs: the Appalachian Mountain Club, the Sierra Club, the Mazamas, and the Mountaineers, respectively. These four pioneering clubs overcame the distances that separated them to cooperate on a range of activities during their early years. As a consequence of this cooperative spirit, they have been able to work together to further the cause of conservation.

Hiking Together

A joint outing to Mount Rainier in 1905 brought together members of the Appalachian Mountain Club, the Mazamas, and the Sierra Club. The Mazamas' historian, in the 1905 issue of *Mazama*, notes that "a sizable contingent of twenty-seven Appalachians put forth the energy to travel across the continent to take part in the expedition. . . . Nor can the Mazamas forget the bright good fellowship and chivalrous mettle of its guests from the Appalachian Mountain Club . . . . May they come often to Mazama campfires." An AMC account of the trip, in the 1906 issue of *Appalachia*, states that "the evenings about the great campfire were given over to song and jest, good fellowship and the interchange of experiences . . . . One night the Sierrans and Appalachians, clad in fantastic costumes made up from their camping outfits, marched down to the Mazama camp, an eighth of a mile below. Borne at the head of the procession was a goat's head fashioned from the distorted root of a tree, and labeled, 'the original Mazama.' Two evenings later, the Mazamas, dressed as a tribe of Indians with faces painted and camping blankets of different colors about their shoulders, came up to our camp to return the visit."

Participants in this joint trip to Rainier were aware that the cooperative relationship they were establishing could have implications for the future of mountaineering and of conservation in general. A contributor to *Appalachia* wrote in 1906 that "the general hilarity that prevailed and songs and ten-minute speeches by members of the three clubs went far to cement a union that it is hoped will prove in the future a powerful factor in the furtherance of American mountaineering and a love of the mountains and the woods by others who may follow."

This sense of fraternity extended to the Mountaineers of Seattle. In 1907, invitations to join the Mountaineers' first outing was "extended to members of all recognized mountain clubs recommended by their secretaries, who will be enrolled for the outing on the same basis as members of the Mountaineers." In suggesting that its members visit the western mountains, *Appalachia* advised its readers in its 1911 issue to "[t]ake a good comrade, or cast your lot with the Sierra Club, the Mountaineers or the Mazamas, where you will be welcome and will find the best outdoor companionship in the world. Nowhere do more interesting people gather in a more interesting way."

Also in 1911, two AMC members reported in *Appalachia* on the atmosphere of another joint outing between the Mountaineers, the Mazamas, and the Sierra Club: "Emerson and I bade farewell to the Mountaineers amid cheers for our club, with recollections of delightful companionship, glorious campfires, beautiful flowers, tremendous scenes, and departed for the Mazama camp on the southwest slopes of Mt. Baker."

This bonding process continued in later years. In 1913, announcement of an outing through the Olympic Mountains "brought Appalachian, Mazamas, and Sierra recruits to join the outing of the Seattle Mountaineers." Here again the sense of fellowship was explicit: "Each camp brought closer the day that dawns early in every outing, when, with strange faces grown familiar and old companionships renewed, the haphazard acquaintanceships of fellow travelers becomes the friendly fellowship of the open trail."

Shared Images

These growing organizations were also unified by their appreciation of the way photography could capture the beauty of mountain scenery. The March 1894 issue of *Appalachia* reports that:

> A successful exhibition of [Vittoria] Sella's photographs of mountain scenery was held in May at the Gallery of the Boston Art Club. The attendance was very large, and the photographs were highly praised from an artistic and educational as well as mountaineering standpoint. The collection is now the property of the club, and arrangements are being made for its exhibition in other cities, thus bringing revenue to our treasury and credit to our reputation. [247]

In May 1895, the "Secretary's Report" in the *Sierra Club Bulletin* states, "It is to be hoped that during the coming fall the kind offer of the Appalachian Mountain Club to allow us to exhibit their photographic views may be accepted and that a public exhibition may be held." The "Report of the Committee of the Sella Collection" in the January 1896 issue of *Appalachia* includes a brief discussion of the arrangements being made to loan the picture collection to the Sierra Club. The committee members state that the exhibit "might at any time be called for by our California friends."

In October 1896 the collection was forwarded to San Francisco, where it was exhibited for ten days under the auspices of the Sierra Club. "The exhibition was visited by some 1,360 persons, and was highly appreciated."

Early in May 1897, the Sella Collection was sent to Oregon to be exhibited by the Mazamas, and "was for many weeks the object of widespread interest in that mountaineering center." The collection was also lent to two smaller mountain clubs, the Rocky Mountain Club of Colorado, and the Green Mountain Club of Vermont.

In 1898, after receiving the loan of the Sella Collection, the Mazamas sent their own collection of photos to the AMC. With appreciation mixed with evident local pride, an author commented in the 1898 issue of *Appalachia*, volume nine, "From exhibits thus made, many fine photographs of the scenery of the Pacific States have been presented to our club as some slight return for the loan of the Sella views." Similarly, in 1899, a prominent member of the Sierra Club, Professor J. N. LeConte, presented the AMC with "thirty Sierra photographs from negatives," which were bound together with several presented by him the year before.

Role Models

Credit for beginning the Sierra Club High Trip tradition must be given in part to the AMC and the Mazamas. In 1901, the *Sierra Club Bulletin* states that "[a]n excursion of this sort, if properly conducted, will do an infinite amount of good toward awakening the proper kind of interest in the forests and other natural features of our mountains, and will also tend to create a spirit of good-fellowship among our members." The author acknowledges that "[t]he Mazamas and the Appalachian Clubs have for many years shown how successful and interesting such trips may be made." Though the Sierra Club had always encouraged camping and mountaineering, the High Trip of 1902 was the first "official" trip sponsored and run by the Sierra Club. After this, such outings became a central aspect of the club's activities, as they had always been for the AMC and the Mazamas.

During the decades before and after the turn of the twentieth century, the West Coast clubs relied on other precedents set by their Boston forerunner. A comparison between the first issues of the *Sierra Club Bulletin*, appearing in early 1894, and of the more established *Appalachia* for the same time period reveals an almost exact similarity in editorial style. As with the AMC publication, which first appeared in 1876, the body of the *Sierra Club Bulletin* consisted of a series of accounts of mountain exploration trips accompanied by full-page photographs of the mountain scenes being described.

The Sierra Club's description of the AMC's publication is clearly complimentary. *Appalachia* trip reports are described as "interesting" and "well illustrated." The photographs are described as "fine." J. M. Stillman, who wrote a piece for the *Bulletin*, concluded that the AMC's journal was "surely a creditable showing of its life and activity." In June 1903 the *Sierra Club Bulletin* noted that it hoped to match *Appalachia*'s high standard of excellence for mountaineering publications.

Mourning Phillip S. Abbot

In the record of early cooperation among American mountain clubs, one story of particular drama and poignancy stands out: the first fatal accident in the twenty-year existence of the AMC, which took the life of a young climber named Phillip S. Abbott on August 3, 1896, in the Canadian Rockies. Both the AMC and the Sierra Club reported on the accident, emphasizing Mr. Abbot's mountaineering skills and his interest in bringing the two clubs closer together.

An ardent mountaineer, Phillip Abbott had devoted himself to establishing closer relations between members of the AMC and the Sierra Club. A contributor to volume eight of *Appalachia* in 1896 writes: "To work more effectively toward this end, he had himself joined that society [the Sierra Club], which mourns his loss with us, and in a visit to San Francisco last May, had consulted with some of its leaders as to the possibility of a greater concert of action between the two organizations." It was in the view of what he believed *Appalachia* might accomplish toward this end that Abbott contributed his energy to that publication.

The *Sierra Club Bulletin's* detailed account of Phillip Abbot's fatal climbing accident included a tribute to Abbott's life. The story was illustrated with the same picture of the youthful Abbott that had been used in *Appalachia*. The *Bulletin* makes note of the *Appalachia* article, which "gives a graphic account of the excursion in which our fellow-member, Mr. P. S. Abbott, lost his life."

Political Activity

Fostered by joint participation in hiking outings, the sharing of photographs and information, and a common enthusiasm for the outdoors, mountain club cooperation eventually expanded into the political arena, where the clubs pooled their efforts in a number of conservation battles during the early twentieth century.

Even before this, in 1897, the Sierra Club joined with the AMC, the American Association for the Advancement of Science, and the Geological Society of America to work toward the establishment of a national park at Mount Rainier. A bill based on their efforts was presented in the U.S. Senate by Senator Squire of Washington and became law in 1899.

The joint outing to Mount Rainier in 1905 was, in fact, not all fun and games. At a meeting during this trip, participants unanimously adopted a resolution to appoint a committee representing those present "to report to the President of the United States and to the Secretary of the Interior, on the present condition of this National Park, and to recommend such action for its betterment as might appear desirable." The joint resolution was presented by the Sierra Club as a "disinterested expression of the views and recommendations of nature lovers and mountaineers."

A few years after this outing, the Sierra Club, the Mountaineers, and the AMC participated in one of the major events in the history of American conservation: the effort to save the Hetch-Hetchy Valley from being flooded to create an increased water supply for the city of San Francisco. Although the conservationists were not successful in saving Hetch-Hetchy from the flood of dammed waters, the conflict reinforced conservation as a national issue. Though John Muir and the Sierra Club led the campaign, both the AMC and the Mountaineers contributed their support. The AMC held a special meeting at Huntington Hall in Boston in January 1909, at which about 450 people were present. According to an account of the meeting in the July edition of *Appalachia*:

> Professor William F. Bade, of the University of California, and a director of the Sierra Club, gave an illustrated lecture on the Hetch-Hetchy Valley and the Yosemite National Park. The lecturer emphasized the undesirability of allowing San Francisco to secure through act of Congress the title to certain lands within the National Park for water-supply purposes. [168]

At the conclusion of the talk, the AMC voted that the president be authorized to send a delegate to Washington to appear before the Public Lands Committee of the House of Representatives. The next issue of *Appalachia* confirmed that "the influence of the club had been exerted" "for the preservation of the Hetch-Hetchy Valley" and that "delegates have been sent to Washington to represent the Club at a hearing before the committees of Congress."

At the Mount Rainier gathering of 1905, the Mazamas had noted that the representatives of the AMC were somewhat "staid" around the campfire. While this may be true, the AMC's representative before the Committee of Public Lands of the House of Representatives on January 9, 1909 made an effective delegate to the halls of power in a way the more carefree Mazamas or Sierrans might not have. Mr. Edmund A. Whitman introduced himself to the congressional committee by stating:

> I am an attorney in Boston, Mass., and I am here to represent the Appalachian Mountain Club, an organization of some 1,600 individuals who are scattered throughout 22 states of this Union, with the District of Columbia; and I was authorized and directed to appear before you at a meeting of the club held when about 400 persons were present. I am present here also at the request of some members of the Sierra Club of San Francisco and California to represent their views. [House Committee on Public Lands, San Francisco and Hetch-Hetchy Resevoir: Hearings on H.J. Res. 223, 60th Cong., 2nd sess., 9 January 1909, 5.]

Mr. Whitman presented a detailed legal argument on why the Hetch-Hetchy Valley should not be flooded to provide water to San Francisco. He also explained that he had become familiar with the region on a hiking trip he had taken with the Sierra Club. At the conclusion of the hearing, the chairman noted that the committee had "received many communications in the form of letters and telegrams from the Appalachian Club and various civic associations and forestry associations both East and West, in opposition to what they assume to be the intended legislation."

Legacy

Early members of the AMC, the Sierra Club, the Mazamas, and the Mountaineers were separated by long distances. Nevertheless, their members shared an appreciation for the beauty of wilderness, and the "fellowship of the open trail." Bonds of companionship forged around the campfire served political purposes as well as the spirit of adventure. They enabled club members to work together in pragmatic and effective ways on pivotal battles of the early conservation movement in the United States, a cause to which they have remained dedicated.

JOSH GREENFIELD holds a B.A. degree from Cornell University and an M.A. degree in history from the City University of New York (CUNY). He lives in New York City.

Allagash Stream

hurries to bloom
in the white tufted waves
of Chamberlain Lake.
Not too many easy turns
after we commune with three
white-tailed deer feeding
on swamp grass off
our port gunwale, swells

of current below the bow deck
churn the peaceful surface.
Not many turns more
by stumps and branches before
curls at shoreline and
splashes over ledge
force us to an eddy. From there
we haul, rope around waist,

against the knee-deep rush.
A few more bends and
a torrent crashes below a bridge.
In another eddy we
secure the canoe,
scramble through stiff
swamp grass dotted with purple lilies
to a rainbow of flowers beside the road.

Back down the quick way
through shoots and scummy cones,
we dodge mossy rocks,
flower petals misted in our hair.

Parker Towle

PARKER TOWLE is an editor at *The Worcester Review*, and a board and faculty member at the Frost Place and Festival of Poetry in Franconia, New Hampshire. Neurologist with the Dartmouth-Hitchcock Medical Center, with a practice centered in Littleton, New Hampshire, Dr. Towle awakes each morning to sun cresting the Kinsman ridge in the Easton Valley.

Olympic Peninsula

I move away, move closer, moved by
the blue familiar spruce, western cedar,
and walnut fruit the squirrels stow.

By my side the shadows of two children
linger. Though grown, they have moved
me to the center of myself. All the love

in the world runs like a river. I feel my way
on the surface of an ordinary day.
The spider in the corner worries into dark,

the dormouse listens under ivy leaves.
The sea and mountains move
and when the mover gathers all I own,

I will look for the limpet, moon snails,
and white stones hidden in sand. I will
taste the salt air and silence, I will see

what is waiting, what is curled in the spiny
bonnet shell, what quickens the velvet ants
in their burrows. Streams run from the hills,

patterns shape on the dunes,
in tangled threads of lapping foam,
another ring of cowrie.

Kay Mullen

KAY MULLEN is a resident of the Olympic Peninsula, "a village in the woods by the bay" where nature abounds. She is the author of a first book of poems, *Let Morning Begin*. Her work has appeared in *Women Writing Journal*, *Pontoon: Floating Bridge Press Anthology*, *Avocet*, *Antigonish Review*, and others.

Hiking Back in Time

In the Mountain Stronghold of Cochise

Barbara Johnson
and Christopher Johnson

IN THE WESTERN UNITED STATES, the past is always present, waiting around every turn in the trail, lurking behind every approaching hill,
ready to pull us back in time. In the Dragoon Mountains, an isolated range of
7,000-foot mountains ninety miles southeast of Tucson, the past does more
than wait; it permeates the air. In this range's magnificent canyons, one sees
few signs of modern life; there are no telephone wires, no satellite dishes. The
past inhabits a silence broken only by the call of a bird or the rustle of a chip-
munk in the underbrush, as one hikes along utterly deserted trails in these
rugged and remote mountains.

Here the past becomes even more palpable because somewhere, in an
unknown crevasse, the great Apache chief Cochise lies buried. One hundred
and thirty years ago, these mountains were Cochise's stronghold, a sanctuary
and fortress for the chief and the Chiricahua band of Apaches who, from 1861
to 1873, waged war against American settlers and eluded the U.S. Army. No
one knows today which of the hundreds of crevasses holds his remains. Yet his
warrior presence still pervades these mountains and canyons.

We arrive here accidentally. Heading along I-10 to another destination,
we see a small highway sign with the words "Cochise Stronghold." Vague,
patchy memories of Cochise eluding the U.S. cavalry in his stronghold for
years compel us to turn off and go exploring. We drive south on Arizona highway 191, skirting the western edge of Sulfur Springs Valley. To our left, we
see the outline of an ancient lake that is now dry; every spring, thousands of
cranes return to the seasonal waters that briefly cover the land. Beyond, to the
east, the alkali flats of the valley stretch for forty miles to the Chiricahua
Mountains. The valley's scrub and sagebrush have been baked brown by the
incessant Arizona sun.

We turn right onto a gravel road with a washboard surface for an eight-mile journey to the Dragoons, which cut a jagged profile against the crystal blue sky as their desolate ridges rise and drop. Standing guard at the foot of the mountains are enormous cream-colored boulders. For a moment we are afraid that the road will crash directly into those guardian boulders, but suddenly it curves left around them, enters a canyon, passes a handful of residences, and ends at a nearly deserted campground. At the trailhead into the stronghold, we see a monument that reads:

Chief Cochise
Greatest Of Apache Warriors
Died June 8, 1874
In This His Favorite Stronghold

It is at this instant, on the edge of the stronghold, that geography and history begin to intersect. Towering canyon walls surround us. The silence is profound, but then the mountains slowly begin to speak. A breeze whispers through the leaves of the surrounding sycamore and walnut trees and stirs the dry brush that carpets the canyon. High overhead, a crow caws.

The trail begins by winding through a desert garden of alligator juniper, yucca, and prickly pear. It heads south along a dry riverbed and enters a

Hundreds of boulders arranged in unique formation line the trail through the East Stronghold.

Tall outcroppings of rock guard the West Stronghold, where Cochise and General Howard negotiated a peace.

Photo by Christopher Johnson

canyon that winds through the eastern section of the stronghold and gradually bends to the northwest. The sides of the canyon are steep and lined with more of the boulders, which stand like sentries as we venture farther into the stronghold and further from today. In this canyon and the smaller canyons that diverge from it like tentacles, one can easily get lost.

To walk this trail is to gain a more intuitive understanding of the Chiricahua people—to see reflected in this wild topography their fierce desire to remain free. To walk here is also to gain a deeper insight into a key piece of history that unfolded here in 1872, when General Oliver Otis Howard of the U.S. Army journeyed to negotiate a peace with Cochise that finally ended the Apache Wars, which had been spreading violence throughout Arizona for the preceding twelve years.

The conflict between the Chiricahua and the United States ignited in 1861 with a series of bungled events known as the Bascom Affair. On February 4, 1861, Second Lieutenant George N. Bascom summoned Cochise to his tent at the army encampment in Apache Pass, some forty miles east of the Dragoons, and accused him of kidnapping Felix Ward, the adopted son of an American rancher (Roberts, 22–23). Cochise responded that the accusation was false and gave his solemn word that he would do all he could to have the boy returned to his father. Historians believe that Cochise was telling the truth and that Ward probably had been kidnapped by a different band of Apaches (Sweeney, *Cochise* 146). Bascom, who had no experience with Indians and knew nothing of Cochise's reputation for honesty, insisted on holding the chief and his party (Cochise's wife, brother, two nephews, and two children) as prisoners until the boy was returned (Roberts, 22). Cochise quickly grasped a hidden knife, slashed a gash in the tent, and escaped. Over the next several days, the chief took several Americans hostage and, after fruitless negotiations, killed four of them. In retaliation, the army hanged Cochise's brother, his two nephews, and three Apaches who had recently been captured while rustling cattle (Roberts, 28).

When Cochise heard of the hangings, he became enraged and swore revenge against the U.S. Army and American settlers. From 1861 to 1870, the Chiricahua attacked wagon trains, ranches, and settlements in the territory. Historians estimate that during this period, the Apaches killed approximately 400 Americans and Mexicans (Roberts, 55). The battles took an enormous toll on the Chiricahua people as well. In 1869, Cochise told an Army officer, "The Americans killed a good many. I have not one hundred Indians now. Ten years ago I had one thousand" (*Arizona Miner*, March 20, 1869). By the late 1860s, Cochise realized that, if his people were to continue to exist, he would have to reach some kind of peace agreement with the U.S. government.

Photo by Christopher Johnson

The Chiricahua Indian Reservation agency was in Apache Pass, 40 miles east of Cochise Stronghold. The ruins of the agency recently were excavated.

In 1872, President Ulysses S. Grant intervened in the crisis and tapped General Oliver Otis Howard, a hero of the Civil War, to negotiate with Cochise. Howard was a deeply religious and humane man, known as the Christian Soldier during the war. Howard empathized with the plight of the American Indians, an attitude that set him apart from other Army officers of the time. His mission was clear: to make peace with Cochise and the Chiricahua.

That year, Howard journeyed to Arizona with his trusted young aide, Lieutenant Joseph Alton Slade. In late summer, they arrived in southeastern Arizona, where Howard learned of Cochise's whereabouts in the Dragoons from Tom Jeffords, the Indian scout who had formed a close friendship with the chief. When the general asked Jeffords to take him to Cochise, Jeffords agreed to do so if no soldiers accompanied them (Howard, 188).

The expedition was arduous, as the small group, which included only Howard, Sladen, Jeffords, and two Apache guides, crossed the desolate flats of western New Mexico and eastern Arizona. They crossed the Chiricahua Mountains, with their beautiful forests of ponderosa pine, and traversed the Sulphur Springs Valley, which Howard noted "was a broad, dry, sagebrush stretch of country" (Howard, 197).

In September, the small company reached the eastern stronghold, where we are now standing. We have walked about a mile into the stronghold on trails that date back to the time of the Chiricahua, and we sit to rest by a spring and wonder aloud if this is the same spring that General Howard described as "abundant . . . a rivulet of clear, cool, most acceptable water" (Howard, 199). The water is now stagnant and brackish. We talk about how Cochise's stronghold was the only place where the negotiations between the two men could have been successful. Because of its remoteness, it was the perfect place for two men to meet each other as individuals, set aside their cultural roles, and earn each other's trust.

Following a dry river bed, we climb another mile to Half Moon Tank, a small reservoir that reflects the surrounding canyons in its quiet waters. We are surrounded by tall, irregular rocks, balanced one upon the other and backed by towering cliffs. We sense we are being watched. It is not an uneasy feeling—more like a heightened awareness that is somehow drawing us into closer communion with the spirits of this extraordinary place. We look up at two enormous rock pillars that appear to have heads, shoulders, and torsos, and one head is bent toward the other in a gesture of supplication and empathy. Further along stands another cluster of rocks that resemble an entire family, with the mother and father on either end and their children between them. Like a family, the rocks look alike yet have distinctive shapes. The parents lean protectively over their children, who speak to each other in a silent language about their adventures that day in the twisting canyons. The mother cradles two infants. This one has a cleft in the top of its head, that one, a fissure all the way down, nearly dividing it into two. Another has thin legs that rise into a sturdy torso and broad shoulders.

Most distinctive is the mother. Her face is square and angular, her jaw strong and confident, her nose flat, her shoulders broad and strong. Her arms reach out to prevent the young children from tumbling down the steep canyon walls. These rock-ghosts cast a spell, as if time has been frozen, as if the Chiricahua who once populated the stronghold have been turned to stone and will remain here for eternity. Later, we will compare a picture we take of this place with a photograph taken years earlier of Cochise's eastern camp and find that they match perfectly.

After another mile of climbing, we reach the divide, a ridge that separates the eastern sector of the stronghold from the western sector. As we stand at this, the highest point on the trail, we see how Apaches could keep watch over

Half Moon Tank reflects the rugged terrain of Cochise Stronghold.

Photo by Christopher Johnson

the entire region, up to a distance of forty miles. Warriors could see the dust raised by cavalry riding across Sulfur Springs Valley from Camp Bowie to the east or across San Pedro Valley from Fort Huachuca to the west. It becomes clear to us how the Chiricahua could resist the army for so many years.

The two-mile descent into the western stronghold begins with a series of steep switchbacks that descend into a rock fortress. The western stronghold, which is much less frequently traveled by hikers today, feels very different from the eastern sector. It is dominated by a large valley with a flat bottom that is well protected from the weather. Groves of oaks and alligator junipers are interspersed with open areas; it was here that Apache families established camps. Throughout the valley are plentiful agave plants, which the Chiricahua used for food and for their strong fiber. High-reaching domes surround the valley and afford views toward the west and the north that are as far-reaching as those in the eastern stronghold.

The negotiations between Cochise and Howard took place here, in the western stronghold. General Howard initiated the negotiations by offering the Chiricahua a reservation in New Mexico at Cañada Alamosa, which would include all of the different Apache tribes. But Cochise did not want his people closed up on a reservation, particularly one that was so far from their homeland. The chief made an alternative proposal: that the Chiricahua receive Apache Pass and its surrounding territory. If they received this land, Cochise promised that no one's property would be taken by Indians (Howard, 207).

At that point, the negotiations were deadlocked, for Howard continued to insist on moving the Chiricahua to Cañada Alamosa. Cochise said he wanted to call in his subchiefs for a council, and Howard agreed to return to Fort Bowie to warn the cavalry not to fire on Cochise's warriors as they rode to the stronghold. Cochise accompanied Howard to the end of the canyon in which they had been meeting, and the Chiricahua chief paused and gazed at the landscape. After a few moments, he turned to Howard and exclaimed, "*Shicowah!* — "My home!" (as quoted in Howard, 209). The two men, who had grown to trust each other through the days of negotiations, then parted ways.

After completing his mission at Fort Bowie, Howard returned to the stronghold, where he, Sladen, and Jeffords awaited the arrival of Cochise's captains. They finally arrived and emphatically rejected removal to New Mexico. Howard, though, was determined not to allow the chance for peace to slip away; he modified Cochise's original proposal, offering a reservation that would stretch from the western part of the Chiricahua Mountains, across Sulfur Springs Valley, to the Dragoons (Howard, 219). The proposal encompassed much of the Chiricahua homeland, and Cochise and his warriors agreed to consider the offer. They retreated to a ceremony in which they consulted the spirits and ultimately decided to agree to the reservation, with Tom Jeffords as the agent.

The reservation, though, was fated to last only a few years, undermined by economic interests that pressured the government to remove the Apaches and open up southeastern Arizona to mining and ranching. General George S. Crook, the commanding officer of the troops in Arizona, regarded the Chiricahua reservation as an unjustified giveway to Cochise and lobbied the federal government to disregard Howard's treaty and remove the Chiricahua (Sweeney, *Cochise* 376). Moreover, young warriors of the Chiricahua and other Apache bands played into the hands of Crook and other opponents of the reservation by raiding ranches and towns across the border in Mexico.

Although Cochise made efforts to stop the raids, the government quietly began to plan the removal of the Apaches from southeastern Arizona. In 1874, Levi Edwin Dudley, the superintendent of Indian affairs in New Mexico, traveled to the Dragoons to gauge Cochise's reaction to the idea of removal (Sweeney, *Cochise* 391). Dudley rode with Jeffords to the Dragoons, where they found Cochise to be very ill, probably from stomach cancer (Sweeney, *Cochise* 395). In spite of his failing health, the chief remained strong in spirit, and when Dudley raised the subject of removing the Chiricahua to New Mexico, Cochise replied that he wished to live out the rest of his days in his stronghold. Dudley convinced the government to set aside plans for the relocation of the Chiricahua for the time being.

Jeffords returned to the Dragoons later that year for what he must have known would be his final visit with Cochise. Reaching the Dragoons on June 7, he went immediately to the chief's camp and knelt beside him. At one point, Cochise looked up at Jeffords and asked, "Do you think we will ever meet again?"

Jeffords answered, "I don't know. What is your opinion about it?"

Cochise said, "I have been thinking a good deal about it while I have been sick here, and I believe we will; good friends will meet again—up there."

Jeffords asked, "Where?"

"That I do not know—somewhere; up yonder, I think." And with those words, he pointed to the sky (quoted in Lockwood, 128–9).

The next morning, he was gone. An observer in Tucson reported that the Chiricahua deeply mourned the death of their greatest leader, whose courage and respect for the truth had bound his people together in their fierce resistance to the forced removal from land on which they had roamed for centuries (Sweeney, *Cochise* 395). Neither Jeffords nor any of the Chiricahua ever revealed which of the Dragoons' crevasses held the chief's remains.

With Cochise gone, the government moved rapidly to break up the Chiricahua reservation, forcibly moving most of the Chiricahua to the San Carlos Reservation (east of today's Phoenix), where the conditions were deplorable. A group of some 700 warriors rebelled against the removal and renewed the war against the United States for the next ten years, until they were finally defeated in 1886. The leader of that last band of insurgents was Geronimo (Roberts, 157).

As we hike back through the western stronghold, up to the divide, and through the eastern stronghold, we feel with deep poignancy the fact that the Chiricahua no longer call this stronghold their homeland. Yet their spiritual presence has lived in these canyons for more than 100 years and can be felt to this day. The Chiricahua formed a spiritual bond with this land. It was sacred to them. It is this continued presence of spirit that makes visiting the stronghold today such a powerful melding of past and present. As we walk these trails, the Apache past reaches out, sounding the force of history and telling the story of a people and a leader who drew strength from this land.

Now the day is turning to dusk, causing the shadows cast by the rocks to grow longer and resemble apparitions. We are caught between light and darkness, and a profound silence settles over the canyon. Then, faintly at first but growing steadily louder, the sound of a drum glides through the dusky air and reaches us; it comes from somewhere to the right, somewhere in the eastern ridge of hills that divides the Dragoons from Sulphur Springs Valley. It is like the earth's heartbeat—slow, regular. Deep and solemn voices begin to accompany the drum. The sounds continue to echo even as we drive along the road that twists its way out of this hidden canyon. As the road approaches the exit, it passes a small cluster of houses that remain near the stronghold. One of the houses is very near the dirt road, and from its eaves hangs a wooden sign with four words carved carefully and deeply into the wood: "Apache Spirit Lives Forever."

WORKS CONSULTED

Aleshire, Peter. *Cochise: The Life and Times of the Great Apache Chief*. New York: Wiley, 2001.

Goodwin, Grenville, and Neil Goodwin. *The Apache Diaries: A Father-Son Journey*. Lincoln: University of Nebraska Press, 2000.

Howard, Oliver Otis. *Autobiography of Oliver Otis Howard, Major General, U.S. Army*. New York: Baker & Taylor, 1907.

Howard, Oliver Otis. *My Life and Experiences Among Our Hostile Indians*. Hartford: A.D. Worthington, 1907.

"Letter from Camp Goodwin." *Arizona Miner* 20 March 1869.

Lockwood, Frank C. *The Apache Indians*. New York: Macmillan, 1938.

Roberts, David. *Once They Moved Like the Wind*. New York: Simon & Schuster, 1994.

Sweeney, Edwin R. *Cochise: Chiricahua Apache Chief*. Norman: University of Oklahoma Press, 1991.

Sweeney, Edwin R., Ed. *Making Peace with Cochise: The 1872 Journal of Captain Joseph Alton Sladen*. Norman: University of Oklahoma Press, 1997.

Worcester, Donald E. *The Apaches: Eagles of the Southwest*. Norman: University of Oklahoma Press, 1979.

BARBARA JOHNSON is a freelance editor, writer, and translator based in Evanston, Illinois. A former English and Spanish teacher, she has pursued her deep interest in indigenous cultures by studying, traveling, and living in Native America and Mexico. Her trip to the Dragoon Mountains fulfilled her lifelong dream of visiting the home of the Chiricahua Apache.

CHRISTOPHER JOHNSON is an editor and freelance writer. He has published articles about the outdoors and about nature writing in a variety of magazines and journals.

Undermining Our Best Nature

A Defense of Dysart Woods

Scott Ruescher

TREES FELL IN FORESTS ALL AROUND THE WORLD for many obscure millennia before anyone was there to hear them. No one was in Dysart Woods, either, when in 1995 the oldest tulip poplar tree in hilly, unglaciated, southeastern Ohio—a tree at least 400 years old—was hit by lightning and fell in a spring storm at the edge of the old-growth forest near the town of Belmont. There wasn't a single empirical philosopher around to ascertain that it had happened.

For reasons less metaphysical than this, Mitch Bartels, the second-generation caretaker of Dysart Woods, reports that neighbors of the fifty-acre primeval forest will be keeping their ears open for the telltale sounds of crashing limbs and ripping trunks. That is, if the Ohio Valley Coal Company (OVCC) gets its way. Since the mid-1990s, the company has been planning to penetrate an unofficial buffer zone that has strongly discouraged mining within 1,500 feet of the woods. In March 2001, the company was granted permission from the Ohio Reclamation Commission not just to mine right up to the edge of the woods, but to "undermine" it. Going literally underground, the OVCC would use its iron claws to dig straight down into a coal seam it had located at the edge of the buffer zone.

In 1998 the Buckeye Forest Council and Ohio University (the owner and steward of Dysart Woods) filed a suit—known as a LUMP, for Lands Unsuitable for Mining Petition—and seemed to have won a stay against the plan in the courts. But the developer-friendly Ohio Division of Mineral Resources Management (DMRM) interpreted the petition in such a way as to allow the undermining. In November 2001, the OVCC applied for permission to tunnel through the seam, underneath the buffer zone and between the sandstone and shale layers, auguring out all the coal through to the other end, somewhere beneath or on the other side of the old-growth forest.

The DMRM reviewed the application several months later and replied with a list of public concerns that would need to be addressed before the undermining could begin. According to the Buckeye Forest Council, the DMRM's sympathy with big business is likely to doom Dysart Woods after the OVCC addresses the complaints on the list. Those *subterranean* seams of coal, according to the letter of property law,

In *Dysart Woods*.

Photo by John M. Morgan

are not owned by Ohio University. According to Mitch Bartels and the Buckeye Forest Council, mining them could mean the end of one of the few remaining old-growth forests in the state, not to mention the nation. The BFC thought the DMRM's sympathy with big business was likely to doom Dysart Woods after the OVCC addressed the complaints on the list—and they were right. In August 2003, the DMRM did indeed approve the OVCC's permit D-0360-12 to undermine Dysart Woods, a decision that may mean the end of Dysart's colossal hardwood specimens if attorneys from Ohio University, the BFC, and fellow nonprofit Dysart Defenders do not succeed in putting a stop to the OVCC's plan with the legal appeal they filed in the Ohio courts in September 2003.

The day after the tulip poplar fell, some hikers stopped at the house Bartels shares with his wife, Anne, where Mitch's parents had also worked as resident caretakers. The hikers reported that they had been unable to find the tulip tree he'd told them not to miss—the one marked so conspicuously on the map in the "Dysart Woods Laboratory" brochure. Bartels was incredulous.

Didn't it stand there monumentally, like some pre-Columbian warrior god, at the eastern lip of the deep ravine, as tall as a big church's belfry and to many just as symbolic of something sacred? Didn't the trail on that side of the ridge road, which cleaves the forest's twin ravines, loop around the tree's 64-inch diameter and 150-foot height?

From the site of that former living landmark—now just a heap of twisted tulip tree limbs—the trail winds along to the nearby edge of the forest, and in a sense to the edge of North American time. A sweeping, V-shaped view opens up there. Looking a quarter-mile or so across the dank brook below, you see a steep hayfield descending from a dairy farm at one end of a ridge and a crown of broadleaf shade trees at the other. You are standing where the ancient, uncut wilderness woods meets the mown, though still bucolic, agricultural worksite. It's like standing in the moccasins of a Native North American (some Shawnee, Delaware, or Wyandot hunters might have wandered over this way now and again from the more populous and water-rich grounds of southwestern Ohio) to look at the British pioneers' idea of good nature. With the ancient oaks in the ravine behind you mixed with beeches, hickories, maples, and a few slightly smaller cousins of the late gigantic tulip poplar, you can reflect on the European-born, Bible-bred, mystery-fearing tendency to

Photo courtesy of the Buckeye Forest Council

The buildings on the surface fracture like layers of stone, causing costly or irreparable damage.

tame the forest utterly and have "dominion over nature." This is a perfect time and place to remember that it took very little time for the pioneers to cut down almost all the trees in Ohio—they'd already taken care of forests east of here—and to contrast our ravenous modern use of natural resources to the tradition of using the forest without destroying it.

To hear Mitch Bartels tell it, and to read about it in *Martha's Journal*—the Buckeye Forest Council newsletter—the Ohio Valley Coal Company will undermine the old-growth Dysart forest in both senses of the word if they are allowed to tunnel beneath it.

"It's called longwall mining," says the friendly, frank, 40ish Bartels of the particular method this madness would employ. Though

Longwall "undermining" causes significant damage to private and public property at the surface in coal-rich areas of Appalachian Ohio, as evidenced by this fault-line in the middle of a Vinton County road.

Photo courtesy of the Buckeye Forest Council

not a geologist—he teaches digital photography and Ohio history at nearby Barnesville Middle School—Bartels has seen evidence enough during a lifetime in the area to prove that this method, unlike the better-known "roof-and-pillar" method generally associated with coal mining, renders unstable the surface above the mined veins. "That's putting it mildly," he says. "You can talk to people all around this area who've been affected by longwall mining."

Without the benefit of "pillar" scaffolding that miners use to support (at least temporarily) the roofs of deep mines, and without stable strata of rock in the vicinity to serve in a supporting role, the longwall mining method means trouble for anything above ground. The coal claw scratches away at the vein of coal, dislodging it in chunks and slabs that are now being touted by the Bush administration, with rhetorical bravado, as clean sources of energy. When the vein is cleared out, nothing fills the space it has left behind. The sandstone and

Several residents of Belmont County have posted signs like the one above to draw attention to the subterranean shenanigans of the Ohio Valley Coal Company.

shale on the surface collapse into the space, causing four-foot depressions in the hills. Stable subterranean sandstone and shale strata fracture and fissure, and what Bartels calls the "perched aquifers" between them (long-established and interconnected water tables) shift positions drastically, sluicing the groundwater into newly formed channels. The buildings on the surface fracture like the layers of stone, causing costly or (in some cases) irreparable damage.

Longwall mining's destructive effect sends fresh groundwater, scant enough already in this terrain, springing from the ground in unpredicted places. While ridge-top silos tilt like Roman towers, while ranch houses show sudden cracks in their foundations, while the curving hillside road takes a tectonic turn it never took before, wells run suddenly dry, the water dripping off the edge of the table in a different place from where it did before. Now it might spring forth from the ground in an impossibly inconvenient or utterly inaccessible place, and now the well at the homestead or by the barn may not even come close to tapping it. The denizens of this landscape may suddenly be out of water, out of shelter, and out of luck.

Same for the 400-year-old "mixed deciduous" oak forest, of course, with its already precarious network of roots in the thin layer of crumbly soil on top of the sandstone and shale bedrock.

"You can't miss it!" Bartels said in disbelief to the confused hikers. "You do know what a tulip poplar looks like, don't you?" he'd asked again to see if they were kidding (not meaning to sound so insistent).

Tulip poplars, Bartels explains, don't have to be very old to make an impression. In fact, it's probably easier to identify them when they're younger and not so tall that their leaves can't be seen up in the canopy of the forest. Reaching for the sunlight, they don't mind bolting straight up from a hillside glade, seemingly more perpendicular than most trees to the flat earth you don't see in this part of Ohio. The parallel ridges of a tulip poplar's bark, vertical as the bars of a jail cell or the piping pinstripes of a corporate lawyer's suit, highlight the right-angular relationship the tree likes to maintain to the lumberjack's level. There's no lackadaisical leaning to be seen in these trees the way there is in maples and sycamores, for example—they are strikingly erect. And tulip poplars have unmistakable big and tender light green leaves, bigger than the maple leaves and darker than the sycamore leaves they most closely resemble, and with a distinctly dipped lobe where the pointed tip of both the maple and the sycamore would be—one of five concave lobes of equal depth and smooth-

ness that give the leaf a profile that cannot be confused with another. In early May the leaf is accompanied on its twig by a succulent orange flower, shaped like the Dutch tulip the tree is named for. That's a sight to see for travelers down the winding tar and gravel roads that lead to Dysart Woods. You don't have to have a case of that "high lonesome" feeling, that Appalachian bluegrass music-loving angst, to get relief from a look at these trees.

In the early 1970s, when I was going to school at Ohio University in Athens some fifty or seventy-five miles away from Dysart Woods, southeastern Ohio was

Photo courtesy of the Buckeye Forest Council in Athens, Ohio.

Old growth in Dysart Woods.

known to be one of the prettiest parts of the state. It still is, of course, because it's the only part of the state where you'll find extensive forest, however young, and substantial foothills. But there were stories of environmental degradation, too. Belmont County itself was notorious for its not-so-grand vistas of yet-to-be-reclaimed strip mines and its mythically monstrous mining machine, the Gem of Egypt. (I am still unsure whether Jeffrey Manufacturing, the defunct maker of coal mining machinery where the men of my father's side of the family worked for years, built that monster.)

Evidence of the ill effects of strip-mining on the waterways alone was everywhere to be seen in the sulfur-yellow streams, even in Athens County, which had long since stopped being a coal-mining center. (Holler hamlets such as Carbondale, near Lake Hope, to this day haunt the passersby like ghost towns.) Dusty, unreclaimed tiers of shaved hillside could be seen from the driver's wheel in nearby backwaters. And you could hear from any lay historian in town that the oak forests of the Ohio Valley hills to the south and west of Athens County, in the Zaleski State and Wayne National Forests, had been felled by Union-soldier lumberjacks, turned to charcoal, and burned in the furnaces of cannonball foundries. "When was this pretty woods last cut," you would wonder, sitting on an outcropping along a hiking trail somewhere. Maybe just once since the civil warriors had come through; maybe even twice; but very possible three times.

Some of the many environmentalists in environmentally beautiful Athens strove to stop the strip-mining in its early 1970s heyday. A student acquaintance of mine—an earnest young woman from the Quaker town of Barnesville in Belmont County—was active in the nonviolent resistance to the mining activity. I recall her saying that she had spent a weekend blocking a road to one of the mines. The Gem's ravenous activities were reported statewide, not just in the alternative Athens news. But Belmont County was quite a ways away for a student to travel. It was easier for a person of worried and indignant conscience to work a little more locally.

The Ralph Nader-inspired Public Interest Research Group was already busy with environmental issues in Ohio. The organic gardening movement, inspired by Thoreau, Rachel Carson, the Nearings, and Francis Moore Lappe, with technical assistance by the *Mother Earth News*, the *Whole Earth Catalogue*, and the *Foxfire* books, was well under way. The cooperative grocery-restaurant in Athens was alive and fairly well. A less cooperative but equally counter-cultural natural foods store was flourishing. Students were saving backwoods cabins from the rot. And the hills of Athens County were alive with the sound of music—traditional folk music, mostly, with dulcimer, banjo, dobro, and guitar—and with the sounds of baby-boomer suburbanites from the much more prosperous and settled cities of Ohio going wild about nature.

I saw all that for myself from 1971 through 1975. But I never heard of Dysart Woods until 1998 and didn't go there until May 2001. There was a lot to admire when I did.

There was the steep slope of the ravines, the drama of the descent, and the well-composed view, between parallel tree trunks, of parallel trunks on the opposite slope. There were the gummy cleaver tendrils, also known as bed-straw, crawling across the forest floor like animated garlands in search of fur to cling to; the pale, moisture-loving jewelweed just a few inches tall this time of year, nowhere near producing the coiled seed pods that snap open and spit seeds at the touch; the much-taller mayflowers, one large single leaf conceal-ing the white flower beneath that dangles from the top of the stem. There was the wild violet—enchanting banks of it. There were the foot-long tendrils of false Solomon seal, with tropical-looking leaves opposing each other in pairs. And down on the bank of the brook: the largest single swath of lady slippers—pink and white—that I had seen in my life, maybe a hundred or more of them on the steep bank above a smooth gray sandbar in the creek.

In Dysart Woods on a dreamy spring day, I heard a wood thrush fluting; an ovenbird screeching, "Teacher! teacher! teacher!"; a barking owl who must have been complaining that I'd woken him up. I heard the chattering com-plaint of the nearby squirrel, also upset with me. And I can't say that I loved it, but I also heard the sound of traffic on Interstate 70.

That day the lightning-struck crown of the fallen tulip poplar lay scat-tered in porous splinters of punk on the ground. Its tangled limbs—dream homes for zillions of independent insects, several communities of spiders, and maybe some frisky rodents—evoked the dramatic agony of fallen warriors from a Greek epic or a Picasso painting. But the splintered trunk, uncon-quered at bottom, remained rooted in the ground.

SCOTT RUESCHER works at the Harvard Graduate School of Educa-tion, teaches in the Boston University Prison Education Program, and writes when he's not hiking or working in his garden.

Coffin's Black Spruce Journals

Appalachia Interview and Book Excerpt

Editor's Note: After a half-century of canoeing adventures, first in New England and later in the Canadian bush, Stewart Coffin, an AMC Life Member and a former member of the Canoe and Appalachia Committees, has gathered together his trip diaries and photographs into a book. My Black Spruce Journals *will be published this spring by Natural Heritage Books of Toronto. Included on the following pages is an interview with the author followed by a chapter from* My Black Spruce Journals *about Coffin's exploration of the Dead and Kennebec Rivers. Coffin lives with his partner, Mary Dow, in Andover, Massachusetts.*

Photo by Stewart Coffin

Les Wilson and Shirley Parker running Poplar Hill Falls on the Dead River, 1958.

Appalachia: How did your interest in the outdoors develop?

Stewart Coffin: Both of my parents loved the out-of-doors, but especially my father. He was an ardent camper and backpacker, as well as a self-trained and highly accomplished naturalist. But his one great passion in life was nature photography. Some of this must have rubbed off on me. Also, in Boy Scouts, we placed an emphasis on hiking and camping. I have always considered myself lucky to have grown up in the Pioneer Valley, surrounded by so much natural beauty.

APP: How did you discover the AMC?

S.C.: While an engineering student at UMass, I was very active in the Outing Club and president my senior year. Our faculty advisor, Dr. Marion Smith, was an AMC member, as was my physics professor, George Alderman. Those two sponsored my membership in the Berkshire Chapter in 1952. It was mostly a hiking group back then. Walter Banfield was just about the only canoeist, and there was no canoe committee.

APP: So where did the canoeing start?

S.C.: After graduation, I moved to the Boston area to work at MIT. My first AMC trip was a whitewater canoeing outing in the spring of 1954. Wow, I became hooked on it instantly. Running fast water was almost like trying to solve an endless series of differential equations. On our second run, with the AMC being short of instructors, I was promoted from beginner to instructor. My first beginner was Jane Lewis. We took to each other instantly, and became steady life partners for the next thirty-six years. We both took out Life Memberships in the AMC. I was on the Canoeing Committee for many years and chairman in 1959.

APP: What was it like back then? You must have seen many changes over the years.

S.C.: The total club membership was less than 6,000. Most of the active canoeists knew each other, including those in the two other whitewater canoeing chapters, Connecticut and New York. The standard canoe was the seventeen-foot

Campfire scene on the Moisie River, 1978.

Jane (Lewis) Coffin, 1931–91, admiring Grand Falls on the Dead River, 1958.

Grumman. Life jackets had just become mandatory after a fatality on the Deerfield in 1950, and they were mostly war surplus kapok or inflatables. Paddles were factory-made ash, bought in wholesale lots for $2.50 each. There were just a few kayaks, which were Klepper wood and fabric foldboats, and one inflatable boat rowed by the legendary Rubber Boat Boynton. We made do quite well with what we had. I compiled a history of whitewater canoeing that appeared in the winter 1985–86 issue of *Appalachia*.

APP: How did the Dead and Kennebec rivers come into the picture?

S.C.: From the start, Jane and I were much involved in leading weekend whitewater trips, mostly for beginners, in the course of which we developed many close friendships. After two seasons of running the same few rivers every spring, we started running scouting trips farther afield with our small cadre of like-minded enthusiasts. This was to gather data for what was to become the first edition of the AMC New England Canoeing Guide. I have already told all about this in the December 2002 issue of *Appalachia*. [Editor's Note: The rest of the story of those two explorations is told in the excerpt that follows this interview.]

APP: Most of your book is about trips in the Canadian wilderness. How did all of that start?

S.C.: In 1962, Jane and I ran an abortive trip on the Dead River in very low water, clogged with remnants of a pulpwood drive. From that day on, our attention became redirected to the magnificent wilderness rivers of eastern Canada, and we never looked back. Soon, with three children, Jane became a stay-at-home mom while I continued summer canoe trips in the Canadian bush. She rejoined me in 1973 on the Salmon River, by which time one of our daughters was old enough to come along. All three of our kids eventually became capable canoeists, and we have enjoyed many family trips together. Now the grandchildren are getting started.

APP: Any favorite authors or books you care to mention?

S.C.: Three, and all with a local connection. First and foremost, *The Maine Woods* by Thoreau, and my favorite edition is the one illustrated by a talented artist and former neighbor of mine in Lincoln, Massachusetts, Henry Bugbee Kane. Next, In *Northern Labrador* by William Brooks Cabot, who according to his distant cousin and former AMC president Tom Cabot was known as "Wild Willie." Finally, for the Barren Ground of northern Canada, the classic *Sleeping Island* by P. G. Downes (see book review in this issue).

APP: Any final thoughts as you look back on memories and forward to new adventures?

S.C.: I have been so lucky. My most treasured recollections are not of rivers run but rather of all my illustrious companions over the years. I have had the good fortune to trip with some of the best. Throughout, Jane was the most faithful of them all. Alas, she died in 1991. I now have a new partner, Mary Dow. She and I have recently been on the Allagash and Dumoine rivers, and I may even be able to talk her into one last trip to Labrador, in spite of the black flies.

Book Excerpt

My Black Spruce Journals

Chapter 3: Dead and Kennebec Rivers

Stewart Coffin

THE CONSTRUCTION OF THE MAINE TURNPIKE and interstate highway system brought many more rivers within weekend driving distance from Boston. Accordingly I had acquired topographic maps covering much of western Maine and spent many long evenings with them laid out on our living room floor, looking for canoeing possibilities. The Dead River, which I had not even heard of before, immediately attracted my attention. The maps showed it flowing for fifteen miles through a remote valley with a constant gradient of thirty feet per mile—truly a white-water canoeist's dream.

At the time, I was working at the MIT Lincoln Laboratory. One day in July of 1958, a tall, athletic looking guy appeared in the doorway of my office cubicle and introduced himself as Les Wilson. He said he wanted to go white-water canoeing and had heard that I was the man to see. I asked him if he was gung-ho to drive for five hours the next weekend just to check out a river in Maine. He said he was, which turned out to be an understatement.

The twin sources of the Dead River, the North Branch and South Branch, rise in remote mountainous country along the Maine-Quebec border and then join together and empty into Flagstaff Lake. Below here the Dead River meanders northward for seven miles, drops for thirty feet over spectacular Grand Falls, and is then joined by another major tributary, Spencer Stream. Here it turns abruptly eastward and flows in nearly continuous strong rapids for fifteen miles to The Forks, where it joins the Kennebec River.

When Les and I arrived at The Forks we went to the general store there and asked proprietor Ed Webb if there might be someone who could drive us in, so that we might paddle back down the Dead River. The Maine Woods are mostly one vast tree farm for producing pulpwood, with logging roads everywhere, so access is usually not too much of a problem if you know the way and can get through all the gates. Ed warned us that the river was utterly unrunnable, but if we wanted to see for ourselves perhaps his younger brother Billy could be found to drive us in.

When we finally arrived at the river's edge, just one glance at the splendid rapids was enough. We eagerly unloaded my Grumman and sent doubtful Billy back to The Forks with Les's station wagon. Despite his inexperience, I had Les take the stern because of his size, and all went well. Four hours later, we pulled into shore right next to Ed Webb's store, much to his amazement. The rest, as they say, is history. The Dead River is now one of the most popular white-water runs in New England, and for good reason.

[photo 3-2. Les Wilson and Shirley Parker running Poplar Hill Falls on the Dead River, 1958.]

I had also been studying maps of the Kennebec River, especially the wild twelve-mile stretch below the Indian Pond power dam (Harris Station) known as the Gorge of the Kennebec. The same weekend that Les and I ran the Dead River we also scouted parts of this spectacular gorge by driving in a couple places as far as we could and then scrambling down the steep banks. It looked challenging, but I thought it might be runnable under just the right conditions.

By the following year, Les had found an equally intrepid canoeing partner named Ken Jones, and we figured that the time had finally arrived to explore the Kennebec Gorge. At five o'clock in the morning, July 25, 1959, Les and Ken quietly launched their canoe just below Harris Dam. The reason for the start at crack of dawn was to escape detection by the dam personnel, because we knew that they did not approve of anyone attempting this run and might even try to prevent them.

At this early hour the generators were not operating and only about 150 cubic feet per second was being released. This allowed Les and Ken to easily wade and lift their canoe over the shallow drops and continue on through the gorge. In midmorning every day the generators were suddenly turned on, releasing as much as 5000 cfs in a sudden surge. The fear by the power company was that anyone caught in the gorge might be swept to their doom.

In the meantime, Jane and I had launched our canoe near the mouth of Moxie Stream and were tracking upstream to meet Les and Ken. The footing was terrible because of slippery, slimy rocks, and we made slow progress. In mid-morning, right on schedule, the river began to rise, although not very rapidly down where we were. By that time Les and Ken had already negotiated the rough upper part and were enjoying a fast run down. We met part way and coasted back down to The Forks together.

[photo 3-3. Jane tracking our trusty old Grumman up the Kennebec, 1959.]

Three weeks later Jane and I, together with another couple, John and Darst Tuckerman, put in at the East Outlet of Moosehead Lake, ran some rapids there and paddled down Indian Pond, camping along the way. When we arrived at the dam we found the Kennebec running at 6500 cfs, with all three generators going plus the sluiceway spilling pulpwood down through the Gorge. It was quite a wild sight, unlike anything we had ever attempted to run before. As expected, the supervisor tried to stop us, saying no one had ever before attempted such a foolhardy stunt. However, the other dam keeper, a Mr. Campbell, befriended us and offered to transport our camping gear down to The Forks. We also learned from him that, in spite of their stealth, Les and Ken had indeed been observed starting down three weeks earlier.

By that time I had established a reputation for caution and avoiding mishaps when running canoe trips, and Jane had complete faith in my ability to do so. We spent four hours arduously negotiating the first mile and a half down to the Z turn (which we named on that run) and another three hours to The Forks, lining down many drops and lifting the canoes over in a few places. To this day, it stands out in my memory as one of the most exciting scouting runs we ever made. Nowadays, of course, the great advancements in skills and equipment have made this run routine for canoes and kayaks, not to mention the regular flotilla of rafts. How quickly the times change.

For more information about My Black Spruce Journals or to order a copy, visit the publisher's website at www.naturalheritagebooks.com.

In Memoriam

Martin G. Larrabee

Martin Glover Larrabee, a retired professor of biophysics at Johns Hopkins University with lifelong connections to the AMC, died June 18, 2003, in Baltimore, Maryland.

Born in Boston in 1910, Martin grew up in a five-story brick row house on Beacon Hill, which had been built by his grandfather. Martin's physician father, Dr. Ralph Larribee, was one of the founders of the AMC, serving twice as president of the club and for nearly twenty years as editor of the AMC White Mountain Guide. Several years ago, Martin donated to the AMC the many photographs his father had taken of the White Mountains over the years.

Martin became involved in the AMC at a very young age, hiking White Mountain trails with his father and accompanying him to the Dover Woodlot, where AMC friends would gather. Until the Dover Woodlot shack was destroyed in 1973, Martin was a member of the regulars who met there almost every Sunday throughout the year.

Dr. Larrabee earned his bachelor's degree in physics from Harvard College and his doctorate in physics from the University of Pennsylvania. He conducted research and taught at the Johnson Foundation at Penn before joining the faculty at Johns Hopkins in 1949. He retired in 1975, though he continued to do laboratory research at the university for another twenty-three years.

While pursuing a distinguished career teaching, researching, and writing, Dr. Larrabee enjoyed the outdoors and developed a passion for hiking. In 1970, he began planning, building, and promoting hiking trails in the rugged Hereford area of Gunpowder Falls State Park, the largest state park in Maryland. In addition to trail building, Dr. Larrabee compiled detailed trail records and worked tirelessly to maintain the trails he had constructed with the help of some of his graduate students and his son David.

In 1943, Dr. Larrabee married Barbara Belcher, who died in 1996. The Larrabee family recently purchased a tree at the AMC's new Highland Center in memory of their parents' marriage, which lasted more than fifty years. In 1998, Dr. Larrabee married Sarah Galloway, who survives him.

Dr. Larrabee's essay "Before the Trail: Huntington Ravine in the 1890s," was published in Appalachia in June 1999. An earlier essay about Dover Woodlot, entitled "Woodlot Memories," was published in the December 1973 issue. A brief excerpt from "Woodlot Memories," referring to the destruction of the woodlot shack, seems an apt way to remember Dr. Larrabee's extraordinary life as a scientist and a hiker: ". . . like many of the finer things of life, one must not dwell on the sadness of its ending, but ont he excellence of its greater moments."

This Far

Lying on the current's bias,
a windfall limb is covered in
driftage because every leaf
has lost its own tree. And here's
a pool, clearing house for
darkness and light, for cirrus
like shavings from a carpenter's plane.
Swallows start from their nests
in the bank below me, and
I see now that the opposite
bank, undercut by run-off,
has opened into itself. I cross
from stone to stone as whirligigs
run circles around me. I crouch
at the entrance to the cave
and find the roots of wildflowers
coming through the roof.
Lobelias, mallows, columbines
I have followed the stream this far
simply to stand among —
they're scud from thunderclouds,
they're knobs and knots and star
bursts. It's all one story, then,
roots at eye level
or the earth whole and flowering,
and the creek's calling is to tell that story.

Thomas Reiter

THOMAS REITER, a recipient of 2003 Fellowships from the National Endowment for the Arts and the New Jersey State Council on the Arts, holds the Wayne D. McMurray Endowed Chair in the Humanities at Monmouth University. In 2004 Louisiana State University Press will publish his next volume of poetry, *Powers and Boundaries.*

Chasing Lightning

Fifty feet away lightning strikes—
I feel ions, smell ozone. A sudden torrent of hail
mixes with rain, hair stands on my legs.

Nearby, dead lodgepoles crack and sway,
thunder claps, a vacuum pops my ears.
No duck and cover, just tundra and

trees for lightning rods. A lone runner
in shorts and tank top, I dodge puddles,
hop streams, plunge through bright,

crashing talons. All around, the storm
exhales as it reaches vertigo, spins
dizzily into orgasmic crescendo—

motion, touch, sound. I surrender
to pure, formless power, raise my arms,
tilt my head—inhale.

Michael David Roberts

MICHAEL DAVID ROBERTS has poems in *Chelsea, West Wind Review, Whetstone, River Oak Review, Petroglyph,* and others. In fall 2001, California State University—Fresno named him Philip Levine M.F.A. Scholar. He teaches English at Fresno City College and spends spare time with family in the Sierra.

Letters

Dear Editor:

While reading the superb article, "Up Close With My Old Man," by Douglass P. Teschner (*Appalachia*, Winter/Spring 2004), I couldn't help but smile with nostalgia. In the mid-1970s, in one of our climbs up Cannon Cliff with the eternally good-natured Guy Waterman in the lead, I recall Guy turning around on the talus and warning with a grin, "Watch out for the boulders, the size of them can be indirectly proportional to their stability!"

After completing the climb through the nose of the Old Man, we initiated a quick descent by the climbers' trail, with daylight fading. Again, Guy was in his best humor, literally running and jumping down the trail, hollering, "The exhilaration of the downhill run!" Very dear recollections, indeed.

—George Cartamil
New City, New York

Dear Editor:

The December issue of *Appalachia*, in the article by John Mudge entitled "An Old Man's Legacy," contains an erroneous caption for an illustration that appears on page 39.

The Bierstadts did list a stereoscopic view of the Old Man in their catalogue of 1860, but although this was among the earliest photographs of the Old Man, Franklin White was selling a stereoview of him a year earlier. Your caption is off the mark in stating that the Bierstadt picture was one of the earliest photographs of the White Mountains. Louis Jacques Mandé Daguerre and William Henry Fox Talbot announced their photographic processes to the world in 1839, and Daguerre's invention was first demonstrated in Boston in March 1840. On April 15, Samuel Bemis (1789–1881), a Boston jeweler and dentist, bought a set of the daguerreotype apparatus. During the summers of 1840 and 1841, he took daguerreotypes in the area of Crawford Notch, and these are not only the earliest photographs of the White Mountains, but also among the earliest landscape photographs ever made. This is all the more remarkable when one considers that the White Mountains were not yet a popular tourist destination. It was a decade before the construction of the first grand hotel in the White Mountains and the arrival of the railroad. Several of Bemis's daguerreotypes can be seen at www.getty.edu/art/collections/bio/a1766.html and www.geh.org/fm/bemis/htmlsrc/bemis_sum0001.html.

Dr. Bemis soon lost interest in photography and settled in the mountains, where he grew a long beard and carried a staff, and in later years, he became something of a tourist attraction himself. Travelers reportedly asked their guides if he was the Old Man of the Mountain of whom they had heard. And if he was, then one might say that it was the Old Man who took the earliest photographs of the White Mountains.

—Adam Jared Apt
Cambridge, Massachusetts

[Editor's Note: The caption discussed in this letter should have been placed under the photograph of The Old Man of the Mountain that appears in the same article, on page 36. The photograph is from *Gems of American Scenery* (1878), a collection of stereoscopic views published by Harroun and Bierstadt. During the production process, the caption for the photograph and the caption for the page 39 illustration were inadvertently switched.]

Dear Editor:

I was intrigued to read the article about the Cog Railroad and the reference to Jitney Lewis. By the time I first new Norm Lewis, he was one of three school superintendents sharing Vermont's largest supervisory union out of an office in Derby, Vermont, and certainly no longer afraid of working for a woman. He got the "Jitney" tag because he drove a jitney up Mount Washington before he worked for Arthur Teague. He was well known not only as a progressive school superintendent but as Vermont's premier political satirist "Danny Gore," the last surviving member of the Gore family of Avery's Gore (if you don't get that you don't know much about Vermont's geography), who was not afraid to, in his words, "hose them all!" His homemade hard cider, guaranteed to have more kick than a first calf heifer, was also a famous gift to friends. When he found that I had been the architect for some of the high huts, we formed an instant bond.

—**Benjamin Stein**
via email

Dear Editor:

In the Winter/Spring 2004 issue's article about Forest and Crag there is a picture captioned [with the information] that it is the trail crew of 1918. I believe it is well established that this is the 1924 crew. For a source close to home, you can check the June 1929 Appalachia, opposite page 248.

This picture was taken by a newspaper photographer, so it is in photo archives other than just the AMC's. The club has a letter from one of those in the picture: "Hix" Henrich, in which he describes the circumstances and confirms identities.

Several years ago, a fundraiser used a slide of the picture and said that Sherm Adams was in it. Sherm did trail work for the AMC, but several years before 1924.

—**Ted Brown**
Jackson, NH

Editor's Note: Indeed Mr. Brown is correct. We regret the error.

Editor's Note: The frontispiece photo in the Winter/Spring 2004 issue featured an avalanche site erroneously identified as Huntington Ravine. The photo, used courtesy of the National Avalanche Center, was of an unidentified site in the western U.S.

Accidents

THERE WERE THREE DEATHS in the White Mountains during the summer 2003 season. One was caused by a heart attack, an almost annual occurrence. The other two were painful tragedies with few lessons for us. In one case, a hiker attempted to rescue his dog who was swimming in fast-flowing water; both man and dog died. And in an incident that saddened the entire region, a child wandered off into the woods near his home; a massive search discovered his body a few days later. Besides the one heart attack, there were an unusual number of other illnesses that occurred on the trail. There were also the usual falls, and the lost, benighted, and separated hikers.

While I was visiting the Fish and Game Department in Concord, New Hampshire, Col. Jeffrey Gray, the Chief of Law Enforcement, spoke to me about the department's "hikeSafe" initiative and its website. On returning home, I visited the site at www.hikesafe.com and found a wealth of excellent information and advice. I strongly recommend the site to anyone interested in hiking safely in the White Mountains.

The reports below are based almost entirely on the public record kept by New Hampshire's Fish and Game Department, the state agency charged with responsibility for overseeing searches and rescues within the state.

Hiker Lost in Bad Weather on Mount Monadnock.

On Oct. 26, 2003, Mark A. (19), Zdenko J., and Joanna W. (no ages given) were climbing the White Dot Trail on Mount Monadnock toward the summit. Conditions were bad: Visibility was poor on the summit, it was windy, light rain was falling, and the trails were slippery from rain and fallen leaves. Rangers, both at the gate and on the mountain, were advising hikers to stay on the White Dot Trail and to consider turning around. At about 2:00 P.M. the three hikers came upon a ranger and were advised that, since there were only three hours of daylight left, they should not go to the summit. They apparently ignored the ranger and continued.

When they reached a difficult ledge called "The Chute," Joanna W. decided she could not climb it and descended. The other two continued but became separated below the upper junction of the White Dot and White Cross Tails. Zdenko J. returned to where Joanna W. was waiting, and they reported Mark A. missing. Due to the bad weather, an extensive search operation was mounted. It was misting, and the temperature was between 50° and 60°, with winds out of the SW gusting to 30 MPH. The search failed to find Mark A., who walked out on the morning of Oct. 28 on Lake Road in Dublin, on the other side of the mountain. He was suffering from only mild hypothermia and from being wet.

According to the report, Zdenko J. told Fish and Game's Sergeant Craig Morrocco that, a few days previously, he and Mark A. had attempted to walk to a lighthouse but that Mark A. was unable to get there. He felt humiliated and was determined to make the summit that day.

Comment: The so-called "small" mountains of New Hampshire can be very inhospitable places in bad weather. Mounts Monadnock, Cardigan, Kearsarge, and Major are all easy trips in good weather. Close to populated areas, they are very, very popular. Familiarity may breed complacency, however, and people often forget that weather is one of the most important determinants of the ease or difficulty of any trip. In this case, the decision should have been straightforward. The hikers were told at the gate that conditions were bad, and a ranger on the trail specifically advised them not to attempt to reach the summit. I suppose that it is possible to *understand* Mark A.'s decision, in light of his desire to redeem himself from a recent failure. That does not make it any less unwise.

There is a profound difference between the hiker with marginal fitness, skills, and equipment who continues out of sheer stubbornness and the skilled, well-equipped hiker who enjoys battling what Scottish mountaineers call "full conditions," when arctic winds blow straight over the North Sea into their faces. The former does not understand what he is getting himself into. The latter is fully aware, but believes his skills and equipment will bring him back safely. More important, he knows enough to monitor conditions, ready to retreat when they become unsafe.

Lost Hikers on Mount Washington

On August 24, 2003, Frank B. (45), Rene B. (no age given), Brianna B. (no age given), and Tracy S. (15) set out for the summit of Mount Washington, leaving their overnight gear at the Hermit Lakes shelter. Soon Brianna and Rene B. turned around, while the other two continued up, reaching the summit by 5 P.M. On the way down, they started down a wrong trail (almost certainly Crawford's Path) and saw the Lakes of the Clouds. They realized from their map that they were on the wrong trail and hoped to find the Tuckerman's Ravine trail to their left. They saw a cairn and went off trail toward it, but on reaching it, they saw no further cairns. Since they believed the trail to be to their left, they continued in that direction but descended without finding the trail. By nightfall, they were below treeline and stopped hiking, since they had no light. The next day, they found a brook and eventually reached the Dry River Trail and got a ride back to Pinkham Notch.

Comment: This is a frequent error: heading down from the summit by the wrong trail. In this case, the hikers were very unobservant; Tuckerman's Ravine Trail reaches the summit after crossing a parking lot, while Crawford's Path does not. Hikers must be aware of the number of trails leaving a summit and take the time to determine the correct one for them. Once they realized that they were on the wrong trail, these hikers should have looked more carefully at their map. It is not clear how far down they were at the time, but assuming they were rather high up, they should have continued down Crawford's Path to the Southside Trail, which would have brought them to Tuckerman's Junction. If they were lower down, they should have gone almost to the hut, taking the Crossover Trail or spending the night at the hut if it was too late to descend safely.

If you navigate off trail, you need, in addition to a map, either a compass or a very good understanding of the features shown on the map. The hikers were correct in assuming that they had to go to their left, but they clearly did not go far enough in the right direction. They should have remained hilking along the contour, with no elevation loss. But they continued downhill, probably heading southeast rather than due east as they should have done. Even with a compass, it is very easy to let the slope pull you down when you should be traversing. Unless you have substantial experience navigating off trail, it is always much safer to stay on marked paths, even if that will lengthen your trip quite a bit.

Franconia Ridge Hikers Stray Onto Garfield Ridge

On May 19, 2003, Lindsey D. (19) and Julie S. (18) hiked up Falling Waters Trail, went over to Mount Lafayette and, instead of descending by the Greenleaf Trail as planned, continued along the Garfield Ridge Trail and eventually descended by the Mount Garfield Trail. Around 6:00 P.M. they called 911, saying they had no lights. They were told to descend as fast as possible in the hope that they would get out before dark. When they did not come out around 8:00 P.M., Conservation Officer Samuel Sprague hiked up with lights, meeting them about 1.5 miles from the trailhead at 9:30 P.M. In addition to having no lights, they had no map and no compass; they had been following oral directions.

Comment: Hundreds of hikers successfully do the classic Franconia Ridge traverse with neither map nor compass; in good visibility there is a large sign near the summit of Mount Lafayette pointing the way down to the hut. But a hiker who relies on memorized oral directions is always at risk of taking the wrong trail. Although infrequent, it happens often enough to make a map, a compass, and the knowledge of how to use them essential when hiking on trails that you are not familiar with. I always make it a point to carry my maps and compass—even on trails that I frequent often.

Hikers Surprised by Deep Spring Snow

On May 1, 2003, Zohar T. (17) and Jonathan A. (17) were bushwhacking up Redrock Brook to an unnamed pond, a trip described in Daniel Doan's book, *50 More Hikes in New Hampshire*. The next day, they continued up to the Twinway Trail. When they reportedly became "overcome by snow depths and cold," they called for help by cell phone. The AMC Zealand Hut caretaker retrieved them on Zealand Mountain and took them to the hut for the evening.

Comment: Since the Fish and Game Department was not directly involved in the rescue, the details are very sketchy. But it does serve as a reminder that, long after the crocuses have come out in Boston (and, indeed, in North Conway) there is still deep snow on the less-used trails in the mountains, and it can still be very cold at night. It is important to take along warm clothing as a safety precaution, just in case you hike up to a colder season than the one you began in.

Hiker Attempts to Rescue Dog, Both Drown

On October 17 2003, Brian R. (39) and Elaine R. (37) drove up to Lincoln, New Hampshire, to participate in the search for a young boy (see News and Notes section for details of that event). Since they had a dog with them they were not allowed to join the search, because their pet would have interfered with the trained search dogs. They decided to hike to the scenic Franconia Falls instead. It had been raining for a few days, and the currents in the river were swift. The dog jumped in the stream to swim and had difficulty getting out. Brian R. attempted to rescue him and drowned in the severe currents in the falls.

Comment: This is the type of accident that I find very painful to analyze. It is obvious that jumping into fast-running water above falls is very unwise, even more obvious in retrospect when the fatal outcome is known. Yet it is impossible not to sympathize with the victim. While a pet is not a human, many pet owners have a profound affection for their pets. To stand idly by and watch the pet drown is very difficult. In this case, I fear, it was the only prudent course of action.

Hiker Suffers Fatal Heart Attack

On August 24, 2003, Alva P. (66) was found by a hiker on the Falling Waters Trail seated and slumped over, unresponsive and not breathing. The hiker placed a cell-phone call, which was interrupted, and then descended to call for help, leaving his wife with the victim and his three grandchildren (ages 8 to 11). Two physicians arrived on the scene soon thereafter and administered CPR until they decided it was too late. The victim was known to have high blood pressure but was considered otherwise fit for his age.

Comment: As hikers continue hiking when they reach the age at which heart attacks are common, they will, occasionally, suffer from them on the trail. It is very unlikely that hiking is the cause of these attacks, since regular exercise is one of the best ways of protecting oneself from having them. It is clear from the report that Alva P. was, in fact, fit for climbing. But it's important to remember that "weekend warriors" of a certain age are at risk in the mountains, so regular exercise is essential.

Hyperthermic, Dehydrated Hiker on Mount Welch

On July 5, 2003, Kathy M. (22) was hiking up Mount Welch with no food or water. It was a very hot (90°) and humid day, and she suffered heat exhaustion and dehydration with severe cramps. Rescuers gave her fluids, then started a carry-out, but her condition soon improved, and she was able to walk most of the way without assistance.

Comment: Hikers suffering from clinical dehydration are just the tip of the iceberg. Many hikers do not drink as much as they should on a hot day, yet do not get ill. The few who do are a warning to the others! Individuals differ in their needs for fluid, but there are some general principles to keep in mind: Hydration should begin when you wake up, after a night of losing water through your skin and kidneys. A drink at the trailhead is also useful for the beginning of the hike. As you move along, it is not enough to carry water; you must drink it. You're far more likely to drink if your water is readily accessible than if it is buried in your pack (and smooth round bottles tend to slip to the very bottom of the pack). The new water carriers that attach to the outside of your pack are a good investment. It is also essential to remember that thirst is not a good indicator of need. Drink before you're thirsty.

Other Illnesses

On May 28, 2003, Larry M. (14) was taken ill with severe abdominal cramps near the junction of the AZ and Zealand trails. Initially, the AMC caretaker at the nearby Zealand Hut thought he could arrange a carry-out with the resources available at the hut, but reinforcements had to be called as progress was slow.

On June 26, 2003, Pierce W. (18) and Joshua W. (no age given) hiked up Liberty Spring Trail to the Garfield campsite. Pierce W. felt sick shortly after arrival and was unable to keep food or fluid down. On the campsite care-taker's advice, the victim was evacuated by helicopter the next day. No med-ical diagnosis was given.

On July 29, 2003, Ronald K. (12) was staying at Lakes of the Clouds Hut with his uncle Paul G. (no age given) when he developed vomiting and acute abdominal pains. A doctor staying at the hut examined him and communicated with the medical staff at Memorial Hospital in North Conway. His illness was diagnosed as appendicitis, and he was carried up to the summit and evacuated down the road.

On September 3, 2003, Edward G. (58) was hiking on Mount Crescent Trail in Randolph when he was stung multiple times by hornets and suffered an allergic reaction. He had an epi-pen and had injected himself, then waited until rescuers came and helped him walk out to a waiting ambulance.

Comment: For most people, an insect sting will cause little more than a painful, raised welt that will subside in a day or so. Some people, for reasons that are not fully understood, have developed hypersensitivity from earlier exposure to the venom and have a severe, potentially fatal, reaction to further stings. Once a hiker knows that he suffers from hypersensitivity he can carry an injectable form of epinephrine (adrenaline), available by prescription. That should be followed by oral antihistamines. Evacuation is recommended.

Young Hiker Injured on Kinsman Ridge

On July 23, 2003, an Outward Bound group (eleven boys 12 to 13 years old and two adult counselors) was doing a six-day trip across the Kinsman Ridge. Brendan F. (13) slid down a four-foot rock, caught his foot on a root at the bottom, and rolled his ankle to the outside. The group called for help and made camp. It had been raining quite heavily, and rescuers decided that the conditions were too treacherous for a carry-out. A National Guard helicopter transported the victim to Speare Memorial Hospital, in Plymouth, after he had been carried out to a location where the helicopter could land. One volunteer (Tina M. [41]) slipped and injured herself during the rescue.

Comment: The *White Mountain Guide* describes the Kinsman Ridge Trail as "... a more difficult route than one might infer from the map—footing is often rough, and there are many minor ups and downs." Add the rain, which had made the rocks and roots even more treacherous, and it is easy to understand the decision to use a helicopter rather than carry a litter over that terrain.

This rescue prompted an unusually large amount of discussion on the hiking bulletin boards, long before the official Fish and Game report was released. Much of it centered on why a group, dedicated to self-reliance, did not attempt to evacuate the victim themselves. It seems to me that, with only two adults and ten children aged 12 to 13, the group did not have the manpower to do a self-rescue. Carrying a litter is hard work and needs a large number of people to allow for frequent rotation of the carriers. The authors of *Mountaineering, the Freedom of the Hills* write: "Thirty or more rescuers can be required to carry an injured climber more than two or three miles on even the best of trails."

Technical Rescue on Mount Washington

On October 13, 2003, Anthony V. (38) and Elke B. (28) planned to hike Mount Washington from Pinkham Notch. The report describes them as having limited experience and adequate daypacks but insufficient clothing for an overnight. They went up by the Lions Head Trail and were descending by the Tuckerman's Ravine Trail in mid-afternoon. They lost the trail and decided to descend the headwall on wet and slippery rocks. At 3:30 P.M. Anthony V. slipped and fell. Elke B. was able to call loudly enough to be heard by hikers, who phoned for help. Given the terrain, a technical rescue with ropes was necessary—and rather difficult. Elke B. was stranded and had to be belayed down. Anthony V. suffered a crushing injury to his right ankle and foot and a probable broken pelvis.

Comment: Tuckerman's Ravine Trail is an easy trail that crosses difficult terrain. It manages never to be really steep, and with the exception of a couple of short stretches, has good footing. But while the trail itself is reasonably easy, the terrain it crosses is very steep and rocky, so losing the trail is serious. It is a very clearly marked, however, so it is not clear why this pair lost their bearings.

Bushwhacker Benighted on West Osceola

On September 1, 2003, Paul P. (65) planned a bushwhack to the West Peak of Osceola, followed by a descent to the East Pond Trail. He started at noon and reached the West Peak at 4 P.M. At 9 P.M. he was making slow progress in dense brush and called 911 on his cell phone. On their advice he stayed where he was and lit a fire. Next morning, he hiked out after carefully making sure the fire was completely out. He was well equipped with a flashlight, headlamp, energy bars, water, and a rope.

Comment: The West Peak of Mount Osceola is one of the peaks on the Trailwrights list and is known to few people other than those who pursue that list. It is very difficult to estimate how long a bushwhack will take, as the time depends very much on the bushwhacker's luck (or lack thereof) in avoiding dense brush. By September, the days have started to shorten significantly, so it is difficult to justify a noon start. While hiking on a trail with a flashlight (a headlamp is much better) is perfectly feasible, bushwhacking by artificial light is far more difficult. It is difficult to understand why an obviously experienced hiker would start so late. My assumption (which, I admit, is pure speculation) is that the original plan called for a more suitable starting time, and that he was delayed. If my speculation is correct, the only appropriate action would have been to reschedule the trip. All plans should be considered contingent on a set of assumptions, and if these assumptions do not hold, the plan must be reevaluated.

Miscellaneous Benighted Hikers

In addition to the bushwhacker noted above, six groups of hikers were over-taken by darkness and none had lights with them. Two of the groups where on major peaks in the White Mountains (Adams and Lafayette), while the other four where on lesser trails (Mount Kearsarge, Mount Morgan, Blue Job Mountain, and the Cascade Basin Trail on the lower slopes of Mount Kins-man). I will describe and briefly comment on three of these incidents, then make some general comments.

On September 7, 2003, Timothy G. (38) and Tina L. (33) were hiking in Winslow State Park to the summit of Mount Kearsarge with their children (10 and 11) when they lost the trail in the dark. They called for help as they had no flashlights. As soon as Conservation Officer John Wimsatt reached the parking lot and sounded his siren he heard them call for help, and he quickly escorted them to the parking lot.

Comment: Mount Kearsarge is a relatively easy mountain to climb, but certainly not a trivial one, at least when approached from Winslow State Park (the trail from Rollins State Park is much shorter). Both of the trails that leave from Winslow State Park have 1,100 feet of elevation gain and are over a mile each way. For an experienced hiker, two or three hours would certainly be ample time for the trip, but a family with young children will obviously move more slowly. The report does not state when they started, but obviously they started too late.

On September 20, 2003, Greg B. (17), David B. (17), Brandon L. (18), and Melinda W. (15) started hiking up to Mount Adams at 12:30 P.M. equipped for a day hike. They turned around as the day got late. Beginning their descent by the King Ravine Trail, and were benighted just below Mossy Falls. They had no lights and no extra clothes, but they did have a cell phone that they used to call for assistance. The Fish and Game Department decided that, given the weather and their ages, they would evacuate them that night, and the victims and rescuers reached the trailhead shortly before midnight.

Comment: It is difficult to decide where to start commenting on this inci-dent. Mount Adams is the second highest peak in New Hampshire, and all trails starting from Route 2 are more than four miles each way, with about

4,500 feet of elevation gain. Starting such a trip after noon is completely unjustified for any but the strongest and most experienced hikers (who are very unlikely do so). The King Ravine Trail is one of the steepest trails on the mountain, and hence one of the least suitable for descent as darkness is approaching. One or more of these hikers might easily have had a severe fall had darkness overtaken them while they were still on the headwall. Finally, hiking in the Presidentials at any time of the year without extra clothing is extremely unwise. It is even less wise on the last day of calendar summer.

On September 21, 2003, Steven E. (46) and Margaret H. (43), vacationing from Florida, had hiked up the Old Bridle Path to the Greenleaf Hut. During the hike, Steven E.'s knee started to swell, slowing them down. They were benighted on the way down, they did not have any lights, and their cell phone did not pick up a signal. A passing hiker did not have a spare flashlight but called 911 for them. Later, they met a hiker who did have a spare flashlight, and Conservation Officer Jeremy Hawkes met them a short distance from the trailhead. He found that they had no backpacks, no extra clothes, and no water or food.

Comment: Climbing up to Greenleaf Hut with nothing but the clothes they were wearing shows how completely unaware of the requirement of hiking in the mountains they were. The hike to the hut is 2.9 miles with 2,450 feet of elevation gain. The "book time" of the ascent, according to the *White Mountain Guide*, is two hours and forty minutes, I would estimate that three hours would be a bare minimum for hikers with little experience in climbing. Add a couple of hours for the return trip, and it should be clear that food and water would be needed. Given the substantial elevation of the hut (4,200 feet), the need for some warm clothes becomes evident.

General Comment: Few hikers end up being benighted without a primary cause (injury or losing the trail), which is a testament to the general good judgment of the hiking community. It is easy to avoid falling into that predicament. The first rule is to spend some time planning. Inexperienced hikers can find the "book time" listed in the AMC's *White Mountain Guide* and other good hiking guides. Combine such an estimate with the time of sunset, and add a margin of safety. Do not start unless you can expect to be back in your car before sunset or you are fully prepared to hike in the dark. Planning, of course, implies having the required knowledge. It is imperative to know how long an "easy hike" is before starting it, since an easy hike for one person may be a more substantial undertaking for another.

Then monitor your progress. That is more difficult for inexperienced hikers, who may not realize that they are moving more slowly than the estimated speed for the trip.

Set a turn-around time. Assume that it will take you as long to go back down as it took you to go up. So if you have three hours of sunlight left, plan to turn around after one-and-a-half hours wherever you may be at that time. Since going downhill on steep slopes may take some people longer than going uphill, it is good to add a margin of safety.

And finally, even if you have taken all of the above precautions, bring a source of light (with spare batteries and bulb), some warm clothing, and a bit more food than you expect to eat on the trip.

Separated Hikers

There were eleven groups of hikers that got separated. In four cases, the lost hikers were all adults; in the others, youths were involved. I will describe and briefly comment on a few representative examples, then make some general comments.

On July 1, 2003, Jaroslac H. (44) was hiking with his wife, Slavomira H. (42), their son David H. (15), and a friend of the son, Zachary C. (15) along the Cascade Brook Trail, planning to go to Lonesome Lake. The father lost sight of the boys near the junction of the Cascade Brook and Kinsman Pond trails. The boys remembered that they were planning to hike to a lake, so they followed the Kinsman Pond trail to that pond. When the adults did not appear, they descended and met the rescuers at the parking lot.

Comment: The youths remembered that they were going to a lake, but unfortunately they went to the wrong one. Two things went wrong here. They should have been told more about the planned itinerary, including which trails they were taking and what their destination was. Since they acted reasonably on the basis of incorrect information, they probably would have been able to get to Lonesome Lake with better information. And they should certainly have been told to stop and wait for their parents at every trail junction.

On July 29, 2003, Elika P. (9) was hiking on the Sugarloaf Trail with her parents when she got separated. As she descended, she realized that the trail did not appear familiar. She heard the sound of traffic (from Route 302), left the trail, and headed toward the road. After crossing the Ammonoosuc River, she emerged at the Mooseland Bar and Grill, where the bartender called the State Police.

Comment: If all hikers were as sensible as this nine-year-old girl, the Accidents section would be much shorter! She must have walked more than a mile off-trail to get to the Mooseland from any trail on the Sugarloafs. That she kept going with nothing but the sound of the traffic to reassure her is amazing. That said, she would have been better off staying with her parents.

On September 14, 2003, a group of eighty hikers from a private high school in New England started hiking up Mount Major at 1:00 P.M. and reached the summit around 3:00 P.M. They returned to the trailhead around 4:30 P.M., and only then discovered that four members of the group, Patrick B. (14), Jaime C. (14), Jae-Woo K. (14), and Christopher O. (13) were missing. They had gone down a wrong trail and were found around 6:30 P.M. on another trail. They had apparently followed the Mount Major Blue Trail west to the Corridor 22 snowmobile trail, instead of traveling east on the blue trail to return to the correct trailhead.

Comment: Taking a group of eighty up a mountain is, of course, a blatant violation of Leave No Trace principles. In addition, if most of the eighty are youngsters, it is extremely unsafe as well. Keeping track of a group that size is very difficult. Still, anyone leading a group of youngsters in the outdoors should be very careful to have an accurate headcount before leaving the summit; losing four participants and not being aware of it until the group has reached the trailhead is inexcusable. Apart from the group size, this is another classic "left summit by the wrong trail" story. The eastern side of Mount Major is on a major road, but to the west there is a large area with no roads, and some of the trails that leave the summit head into that area. It is easy to forget that people can get lost in very nonthreatening areas.

General Comment: There are two approaches to the problem of part of a group getting lost while the rest of the group stays on the correct trail: The group can be kept together, or every member of the group can know how to return to the trailhead.

The first approach is the one recommended by the joint New Hampshire Fish and Game and White Mountain National Forest "hikeSafe" program. As they write on their website: "You should start as a group, hike as a group, end as a group." They strongly recommend pacing the hike according to the slowest hiker.

That is certainly the safest way to hike, but there are times when this plan is difficult to implement. The most obvious case is when there are youths, full of energy, hiking with slower adults. In theory, they should accept the pace of the adults, but that rarely works in practice. People hike because it is fun, and hiking slowly with the adults takes a lot of the fun out of the trip. Even with a group of adults with very different levels of fitness, it may be difficult to require the fittest to go slowly, since that will make the trip much less enjoyable for them.

A compromise is to allow the faster hikers to go ahead, but ask them to stop at all trail junctions. That prevents the group in the vanguard from taking the wrong trail at a junction and also provides an opportunity to regroup. One problem is that not all trail junctions are obvious, and if the fast group does not see the trail junction they will not stop there. This can be partly solved by explaining where the trail junctions are, which leads us to the other approach to group management.

The second approach is to be sure that every member of the party knows (and fully understands) the itinerary. That requires that each of them has a map and a compass and knows how to use them. That will obviously not work with young children or complete novices.

When hiking to a summit with multiple trails, all participants should be aware of that fact and should be told clearly that everyone must start the descent *as a group*. A head count at the start of the descent is an obvious precaution.

Common sense can help find a suitable compromise. Children too young to be trusted to find their way alone should be kept in sight of adults at all times. Older children, those most likely to be full of energy, should be given a clear description of the planned itinerary and told to wait at the next trail junction, whose location should be described to them. They should also be instructed periodically to wait for regrouping if the junctions are far apart.

For an adult group, much depends on the skills of the members of the group. But generally the same advice applies as for groups with older children, above.

A variation on that approach is to split the hikers into a fast group and a slow group. When doing so it is essential to be sure that the slow group has some experienced members with it and an adequate supply of emergency gear.

That said, I very much prefer to hike with a group that stays together. As I was told on one of my very first AMC hikes, when the strong members of the group rush ahead, the weaker members are left alone in the rear. Should anything happen to one of them, those most able to help will be nowhere to be found. Mutual support is, after all, one of the major reasons for hiking as a group.

Hiker Uses Cell Phone to Request Information

On August 3, 2003, Briged D. (53), Laurie P. (49), Nancy J. (56), and Carol O. (50) were hiking along the Appalachian Trail starting from the Glencliff area, spending the first night at Orr Hill and the second at the Hexacuba shelter. Carol O. started getting blisters on the first day, but they continued. By the third day, they decided to discontinue the hike and find the fastest way out from the shelter. Their map showed a trail from the shelter to Baker Road, but they were not sure whether the trail in fact existed. Attempts to get information by cell phone from 911 were ineffective, and a call to the AMC got cut off mid-call, with the AMC dispatcher alerting Fish and Game. The three women met the rescue party at the trailhead of the alternative trail.

Comment: The 911 system is designed to send appropriate emergency personnel to victims, not to provide information. It is therefore a good idea to have a list of telephone numbers to call in nonemergency situations. These hikers did eventually call the AMC, which would have found an answer to their question, had the call not been cut off. This should remind us of the fundamental fact of cell phone usage in the wilderness: The cell phone cannot be relied on; it may or may not work.

The question the hikers had is an interesting one. Topographic maps give the best depiction of the terrain but are notorious for inaccurate trail information. Current topographic maps still show the old route of the Osseo Trail, starting at the Kancamagus Highway. The trail was relocated, according to Steven Smith and Mike Dickerman's *The 4000-Footers of the White Mountains*, in 1983! Trail maps are more likely to be accurate if current, but many hikers carry old maps, and trails do get relocated.

Miscellaneous Slips

Fourteen additional hikers were injured during the season as a result of various falls. Ten of them had to be carried out, while the remaining four were able to walk out with assistance. Only four of the accidents happened at scenic spots (two near Arethusa Falls, one near Artists Buff, and one to a hiker wading in the East Branch of the Pemigewasset); the other ten happened on trails. Only one incident seems worthy of individual notice.

On July 19, 2003, Jordan S. (23) was hiking up the Falling Waters Trail with Patrick B. (24) and Jamie T. (23). He climbed up Cloudland Falls and fell approximately 20 feet, injuring his foot, leg, elbow, and wrist, requiring evacuation.

Comment: Waterfalls are among the most attractive of natural features in our mountains. Most hikers are satisfied to look at them, but a few more adventurous ones will find the desire to climb them irresistible. I completely understand that desire, but have to point out the twin dangers. First this involves climbing on steep rocks, the kind it is dangerous to climb without knowledge, experience, and, in some cases, special equipment. Add to that the fact that wet rock is bound to be slippery, and it is clear why we have at least one such accident almost every summer.

— Mohamed Ellozy

ALPINA

SOUTH DISTRICT RANGER DARYL MILLER reports that in 2003, as happened before in 2000, a safe season on **McKinley** (20,320 ft) was spoiled by a tragic air accident. On May 28, 2003, a McKinley Air Service Cessna crashed on the E side of South Hunter Pass. All four aboard, pilot Keli Mahoney, guide Bruce Andrews, a climber, and a sightseer, died. The 2003 season was otherwise highly successful. There were no mountaineering deaths or serious injuries on McKinley or elsewhere in the National Park, and although the total number of climbers was down again slightly — 1,179 on McKinley with 688 successes, and 34 on Foraker with two successes — June 12, 2002, was the all-time record day for McKinley, with 115 climbers making it to the top.

The first continuous ski descent of **Mount Hunter** (14,578 ft) was made on May 15 by Lorne Glick, John Wedon, Armond DuBoque, and Andrew McLean. They climbed to the summit in 12 hours and 30 minutes and skied down by the W Ridge and a gully they dubbed the Ramen Couloir in just four hours. In another high speed effort, Chad Kellogg, said to be in training for a speed climbing competition in Central Asia, ascended the W Buttress in 14 hours and 22 minutes and returned to base camp in 23 hours and 55 minutes total. This may be a record for the W Buttress, but not for McKinley. In 1991 the great Anatoli Boukreev climbed the W Ridge in 10 hours and 30 minutes starting from the E Fork Glacier.

There were new climbs from the Tokositna Glacier. Britons Malcolm Bass and Simon Yearsly made the first ascent of the 3,600-foot S Face of **Kahiltna Queen** (12,370 ft) establishing two separate ice routes in early May, and Pat Deavoll and Marty Beaver made a probable first ascent of a couloir on the N side of **Pt 11,520 ft** just to the south. Another set of Britons, Mike Turner, Stuart McAleese and Ollie Sanders, introduced high-standard ice climbing to the **Kichatna Spires** (normally viewed as a rock-climbing venue) when they made a three day, twenty-one–pitch ascent of an ice couloir on the E Face of the **Citadel**, finishing on May 3.

National Park Service (NPS) South District Staff participated in fourteen search-and-rescue expeditions. With the exception of the air crash mentioned above, most of these involved minor injuries or incipient hypothermia, pulmonary edema, or exhaustion. This relatively benign experience may be the result of the extensive safety and information programs now conducted by the NPS. The fact remains that the use of helicopters for high altitude rescue is dangerous, and it is now perceived that climbers have become too ready to ask for rescue.

Obviously not in the same category of rapidly improving safety is the 6,500 ft NW Face of **Devil's Thumb**. In his article in the 2003 *American Alpine Journal*, Dieter Klose dares to suggest the word that has been obsolete in mountain discussions since the 1930s: unclimbable. Klose may know. He has lived in sight of the NW Face for nineteen years, has observed conditions on the face in every month of the year, and with Mike Bearzi has reached the highest point so far achieved — less than halfway. He argues that because the wall practically never comes into condition even by the extremely loose standards of modern high-risk climbers, and when it does, the weather is unlikely to hold long enough for even the fastest of such teams to reach the top — a climb may never be made. The face has been attempted, or better, approached by an international who's who of wall climbers over twenty-five years. Most did not step onto the face, never seeing even a marginal possibility during their visit. The latest candidates, the Canadian pair Guy Edwards and John Millar, made two trips to the wall. On the first in May–June 2002, they suffered twenty days of bad weather and did not try the face. In April 2003 they visited again accompanied by Kai Hirvonen. Edwards and Millar thought the face was in condition; Hirvonen's gut feeling was that the risk was too high, and he turned back before the reaching the pile of avalanche debris at the foot of the face. Edwards and Millar disappeared up the face one night; no one has seen them since. They are believed to lie at the base of the wall, buried by an avalanche.

Klose is a brave man; he has climbed the NW Face to almost mid-height, and he has used a word not in the present-day mountaineering vocabulary. But history is against him. The use of the word "unclimbable" will in itself attract more attempts. In the bitter phrase of the conservative mountaineering pundit E. L. Strutt, the wall may become "an obsession for the mentally deranged of almost every nation." Strutt, speaking in 1937, referred then to the North Face of the Eiger. The following year it was climbed by four men, none demonstrably deranged.

CANADA

F OUR CANADIANS FROM THE VANCOUVER AREA, three women and a man, made a major traverse of the Fairweather and St. Elias ranges beginning at the Haines Inlet in British Columbia and finishing at a road near Cordova, Alaska. Starting on April 25, 2002, Kari Medig, Merrie-Beth Board, Jacqui Hudson, and Lena Rowat conducted a ski traverse across heavily glaciated wilderness terrain, crossing the Fairweather range, dropping to sea level at Aleksek Lake then reaching Canada's highest peak, Mount Logan (5,952 m) on May 18, twenty days from the start. The ascent of Logan's E Ridge to the "summit col" at 5,640 m took fifteen more days. Bad weather caused abandonment of summit attempts after a single try, and on June 7 the quartet skied down 2,700 m to King Trench base camp. They then crossed the final 250 km—the Bagley icefield followed by mixed terrain of passes and small icefalls. Hudson fell 25 feet headfirst into a rock floored crevasse on day fifty-one, but continued the trek for the final four days in spite of the several fractured vertebrae discovered in later X-rays. The group caught a ride into Cordova on June 18 after 675 km of skiing over an elevation range of 5,700 m and fifty-five days in the wilderness.

Also near Elias and the Canadian-Alaska boundary was a long comedy of errors involving four British climbers, permits for cross-border flights, and Canadian and U.S. customs regulations. It all sorted out relatively well. Geoff Hornby and Glenn Wilks stranded on the Eclipse Glacier, the wrong glacier, by a combination of bad weather and administrative difficulty improved the shining hour by making first ascents of **Peak 3,390 m** via the SE Ridge and **Peak 3,320 m** by the E Face. They also squeezed in a new route on the NNW Ridge of **Peak 3,330 m** then wangled a flight to Kluane on the plane of a scientific expedition working on the glacier. Their partners Alistair Duff and Susan Sammut picked them up after a 1,000 km truck drive from Chitina, and the group talked their way back across the border into the U.S. On May 12 they were flown, legally this time, to the rarely visited Goat Glacier in the St. Elias

Range where they made first ascents of **Mount Lola** (2,707 m) via the SW Ridge, **Mount Jennifer** by the W Face, and **Mount Zaylie** also by the W Face.

Under the heading "Peak Bagging (Female)" we have Canadian Nancy Hansen of Canmore, Alberta who became the first woman to climb the fifty-four peaks over 11,000 feet in the Canadian Rockies when she reached the top of Mount Forbes on September 1, 2002. Ms. Hansen spent seven years collecting the 11,000ers and now is a member of the previously all-male, six-member club founded in 1979 by fellow Albertan Don Forest.

In the Eastern Fjords area of Baffin Island a Russian group made a novel combination of big-wall climbing and BASE jumping on the NW Face of **Great Sail Peak**, intended as a memorial to the late American climber Alex Lowe. After the usual Baffin-Island–epic approach, partway by snowmobile and the last fifteen km on foot relaying all the gear, Alexander Odintsov, Alexander Klenov, Mikhail Devy, and Alexander Ruchkin of the accomplished Russian "Big Walls Project" team and BASE Jumper Valery Rozov spent sixteen days establishing a route up the 1,000-meter face. The route, called Rubicon, is close to the Alex Lowe first ascent of 1998 but is somewhat more direct. On reaching the top, Rozov put on his vaned suit (looking rather like a Batman costume, but more colorful in bright red and yellow) and launched himself out from the sheer face—somewhat on the principal used by flying squirrels. He reached the bottom, pulling his parachute at just the right moment, in a little under one minute.

The acronym BASE stands for **B**uildings, **A**ntennas, **S**pans (bridges), and **E**arth, the four locations that participants in this extreme sport use as launching points. Rozov claims that his exploit is the first BASE jump from the top of a just-completed big-wall climb—the Batman suit and the flying-squirrel soaring also appear to be novel. At any rate, his fast descent generated a series of unbelievable photographs.

CHINA AND TIBET

BREAKING THE USUAL PATTERN of Japanese dominance of first ascents in this area, the two most important climbs of 2002 were carried out by Western teams—one British, the other American. Mick Fowler and Mike Ramsden made the first ascent of the N Face of **Siguniang** (6,250 m) in the Qionglai Range in Szechuan. The mountain (which is easily reached from

Chengdu and is something of a Chinese tourist destination) had been climbed by easier routes at least three times previously, and there were two previous attempts on the N Face.

The route chosen on the steep 1,500-meter face was a basalt dike, completely iced up, forming a narrow ice streak up the face to the summit ice fields. The climb was Alpine style, the climbers carrying a bivouac tent, which they were never able to pitch properly because of the steepness of the ice, merely draping it over themselves at the end of each day for five consecutive bivouacs while they tried to cook and eat, then sleep in hanging or squatting positions. On summit day they had good weather and moved up the snow slopes to the top after seven days on the climb. Their descent was by the unclimbed N Ridge, and the good visibility helped in the endless abseils down a "very steep ridge decorated with Peruvian-style snow formations." The climb was awarded the French *Piolet d'Or* award for 2002, the citation noting that: "These two British men epitomize modern alpinism in their search for the most difficult and unknown routes carried out in fast and light alpine style."

The second major first ascent was of **Sepu Kangri** (6,956 m) which lies in the East Nyenchen Tanglha range about three days truck travel east of Lhasa. The mountain has achieved a degree of fame for the three attempts by British parties under Chris Bonington in 1996, 1997, and 1998. In the final year, the British reached to within 150 vertical meters of the summit to be defeated by a sudden storm. Bonington memorialized his obsessive quest in a book with the ominous subtitle *The Triumph of Sepu Kangri*. In 2002 a six-member American expedition led by Mark Newcomb, and incorporating the Himalayan expert Carlos Buhler made the long truck trip to the foot of the mountain and established a base camp on September 18. Choosing essentially the same route explored by their British predecessors, the expedition, hampered by weather and illness but much assisted by the use of skis, reached a top camp at 6,400 m. At 2 A.M. on October 2, Buhler, Newcomb, and Jordan Campbell set out for the summit. Campbell, feeling that he would hold back his companions, abandoned the ascent after 200 meters. Buhler and Newcomb continued up in the dark on a 55-degree slope. As the dawn broke, it revealed a series of avalanche slide paths, which they doggedly cramponed across.

By 9 A.M. a blizzard had developed, and the pair feared a repeat of the British disappointment within 150 meters of the summit, but they persisted in limited visibility to reach the summit ridge and then the top at 10 A.M. The climbers descended in a white-out to join their four companions at the top camp; then after a rest all descended to Camp 1, again making good use of their skis.

Buhler remarks on the miles of unclimbed peaks visible from the summit of Sepu Kangri, and Eric Shipton, musing on a similar view once questioned the value of an ascent of "one of a range of a thousand mountains that nobody has ever heard of." A recent publication by Tamotsu Nakamura illustrates the technique by which such seas of anonymous mountains are transformed into worthy, indeed highly desirable, mountaineering objectives. Nakamura has made twenty-five exploratory journeys to the area between Lhasa and the highlands of West Szechuan since 1990, accumulated photos and maps, learned the local names (which can be legion), and written a brief climbing history. This last was the easy part, as most of the peaks have not been attempted, let alone climbed. His survey has been published as Volume 4 of the *Japanese Alpine News* (Nakamura is the editor) with forty pages of English text, forty of photos, and thirty-two of maps. The thin volume is available from mountaineering specialty book dealers in the U.S., but most will be satisfied with the major (twenty-nine pages) excerpt with thirty-four color photos and five maps published in the *American Alpine Journal* for 2003. Nakamura's beautiful color photos put a "face" on some of the thousands of peaks, nameless or with pin yin names unpronounceable by many Westerners—and many of the pictured mountains are spectacular, belying the impression that much of Eastern Tibet and Western China contains relatively dumpy mountains, notable only for great absolute height.

The effects of Nakamura's efforts are already being seen in the increased climber interest in his chosen region. But this sort of publicity is not all that is happening in Central Asia. Climbers and other visitors to Lhasa and Tibet have noted the major development of tourism by and for the Chinese themselves in the area. (One visitor to Lhasa in the fall of 2003 noted that Han Chinese on package tours were the dominant visitors, outnumbering both Westerners and the traditional pilgrims.) Economic developments in China have created a class who travel for pleasure, and the government and private enterprises are developing a tourist industry to serve that class. A motor road has recently been built around the sacred mountain Kailas in Tibet to permit pilgrims to make the required circuit (three-to-five days on foot, much longer by the more meritorious successive prostration technique) by bus.

Those who have seen the ubiquitous Japanese climbers and mountain tourists (from a country of 127 million) sweep across the mountains of the world from central Asia to the Jungfraujoch in the last half of the twentieth century may look with some concern on the twenty-first century effect of Chinese climbers and mountain tourists from a country ten times as populous.

Other developments in 2002 were the first ascent of **Shimo Kangri** (7,204 m) on the Tibet-Bhutan border by members of the POSCO (a Korean steel company) Alpine Club. Five Koreans led by Nam Young-Mo reached the summit at 10 A.M. on September 29 via the N Face to SW Ridge after a twenty-two day effort, thus reducing the remaining cache of virgin Tibetan-Bhutanese 7,000-meter peaks by one. Near Gyachung Kang on the Nepal-Tibet border, Americans Mike Bearzi and Bruce Miller made the first ascent of the N Face of **Ngozumpa Kang II** (7,646 m) on May 9. On the descent, the obviously tiring Bearzi fell 600 m to his death.

INDIAN HIMALAYA

THE YEAR 2002 WAS NOT A GOOD ONE in Indian climbing. The effects of the general 9/11 malaise and the threat of war between India and Pakistan caused only thirty-five foreign expeditions to take up their permits, for a total of 108 expeditions including all-Indian efforts. In addition, Nun-Kun in Zanskar, the Kishtwar mountains, and the Kashmir valley area were closed to climbers for the year.

In Sikkim, far away from the area of potential combat, there was the first ascent of **Nepal Peak** (6,910 m) since 1939. Herbert Streibel's DAV Summit Club expedition established a base camp on the glacier below the Nepal Gap and climbed the SE Ridge and S Ridge to the summit, Streibel, Claudia Carl, and Johann Paul Hinterimmer reaching the top on October 21. There were several pre–WW II attempts on the higher Kirat Chuli, and as the easiest route to that summit is from the Nepal Gap over Nepal Peak, these were also attempts on the latter. The first ascent of the highest (NE) summit of Nepal Peak was made by Ernst Grob, Herbert Paidar and Ludwig Schmaderer in 1939 on their way to the top of Kirat Chuli. Apparently Nepal Peak was not ascended again until 2002.

In Kumaon the much sought **Suj Tilla West** (6,373 m) received two ascents in 2002. As is now frequently the case, Suj Tilla owes its status as a mountaineering destination to a photograph—taken by the noted exploratory mountaineer and editor of the *Himalayan Journal*, Harish Kapidia. There are two nearly equal summits: The western is primarily snow and the 21-meter higher east summit is rocky. In 1997 a five-member Indian team reached about 5,800 m on the SW Ridge and then was forced down in poor weather. In 2002 following an unsuccessful try by an IMF (Indian Mountaineering Foundation) team, again on the SW Ridge, an Anglo-Indian group including Graham Little and Jim Lowther established a base camp west of the mountain. The Indian members dropped out with illness, and Lowther and Little found unstable snow on the NW Face. They moved to the S side of the mountain and, starting at 10 P.M. on the night of September 27, forced a line up the center of the 1,100 m SW Face. Reaching the summit ridge, they eyed the slightly higher E Summit, but judged it too far away along a corniced crest. Lowther pushed close enough to the W Summit to claim the ascent, then the pair abseiled back down the route of ascent—fifteen hours up, seven hours down.

On their way out they encountered a large Indian Navy expedition under Lt. Commander Satyabrata Dam, hoping to make the first ascent. The Indians were unwilling to try the lightweight approach of the British pair and spent five days putting a thousand meters of fixed rope up the face. On October 6, Dam and three others started up the ropes from the base hoping originally to diverge to pick up the still virgin E Summit, but they found the slopes there too avalanche prone; Dam retired, but the other three repeated the British ascent. Following several days of snow, a second party repeated the route for the third ascent, but the E Summit remains unclimbed.

In Garhwal, the Indo-Tibet Border Police made what is probably only the second ascent of **Devban** (6,852 m) since Frank Smythe and Peter Oliver climbed the mountain (then known as Deoban) in 1937. Smythe and Oliver climbed from the south up the S Ridge and although there have been three attempts since and the Indian Military claimed success on two of them, the claims are widely doubted. The 2002 ascent was from the east to the S Ridge, which was followed to the top on September 19 by Mohammed Ali, Tashi Motop, Jyot Singh, and Vijender Singh. In Western Garhwal above Badrinath and Mana, the Arwa Tower and Spires complex saw substantial further new route development and at least one first ascent, **Point 6,196** by the 1,100-meter N Face, climbed on May 10 by five Frenchmen from the *Groupe Militaire de*

Haute Montagne headed by Antoine de Choudens. The ascenders want to call the peak "Arwa Crest."

Also in Western Garhwal another notable second ascent occurred in October when Canadians Guy Edwards and John Millar climbed the W Face of **Swachand** (6,721 m) northwest of the Chaukamba Group off the Gangotri Glacier. (The first ascent was made sixty-two years before by Austrians Toni Messner and Leo Spannraft via the S Ridge.) Edwards and Millar started up the face on October 3 and hacked out a bivouac site near the top of the second snow field. After two more bivouacs they headed for the summit on the fourth morning, reaching the summit at 4 P.M. that day. They started down the S Ridge immediately, but had to camp high on the upper Maiandi Glacier for their fourth bivouac. Eating the last of their food for breakfast, they forced their way down to Advanced Base, luckily just in time to avoid heavy snow which turned the face into an avalanche trap. (Their luck did not last. Both climbers died on Devil's Thumb in Alaska in April 2003; see above.)

In the same area four French climbers made the third ascent of **Chaukhamba II** (7,068 m) in Alpine style up the SW Face. Yannick Graziani, Greg Sauget, Christian Trommsdorf, and Patrick Wagnon climbed straight up a 50-to-60-degree snow couloir, largely unroped, making one bivouac at 6,400 m before reaching the summit on the evening of October 4. They bivouacked again 50 m below the summit, then undertook a long traverse of the NW Ridge over intermediate summits to reach Meade's Col where they made their third bivouac. Leaving again at midday on the sixth, they were caught by a snow storm and after wading through a foot of snow on the lower glacier reached Advanced Base at 5 P.M. They received little sympathy from their waiting support staff who started the fifteen-hour walk back to Tapoban the following day.

The Indian Eastern Karakoram was the scene of the first ascent of one of the last Indian 7,000ers in May. (The "last Indian 7,000er" is much like the "last great Alpine problem.") In any event, it was a fine effort. An Indo-Japanese group led by Harish Kapadia left Leh in Ladak and established a base camp on the Teram Shehr Plateau below the Teram Kangri group, on the way crossing the Col Italia for the first time in seventy-three years. Establishing a second camp at the foot of the SSE Ridge of **Padmanabh** (7,030 m) the team pushed a route up to 6,750 m by June 24. At 4 A.M. on June 25, Satyabrata Dam, Hiroshi Sakai, and Hirofumi Oe set off for the summit. Dam could not keep pace with the Japanese and turned back at 6:30 A.M. The fitter Japanese climbed a further nine hours through unconsolidated sugar snow and tunneled through a cornice to reach the top at 3:10 P.M. The tired climbers then forced their way down to regain the top camp at 8 P.M. Further summit attempts were defeated by heavy snow.

The Indo-Tibet Border Police (ITBP) have made a number of important first ascents in the Indian Himalaya. They are conspicuous among Indian military mountaineers for getting the name and location of the mountain right and actually reaching the top of their claimed ascents. This competence and dash has cost the organization heavily. In 1995 on Saser Kangri an ITBP team descending from the summit lost thirteen climbers in an avalanche—the worst mountaineering disaster recorded in the Indian Himalaya. Early reports indicate that in another major avalanche disaster, nine members of the Indo-Tibet Border Police were killed on **Panch Chuli II** (6,904 m) on September 20, 2003, apparently while descending from a successful climb of the SW Ridge (first climbed by another ITBP team in 1973). Among the lost climbers was Sange Sherpa, one of the two mountaineers (the other is his brother Kusang Sherpa) to climb Everest by all three major approaches: the S Col-SE Ridge, N Col-NE Ridge, and the Kangshung Face.

NEPAL HIMALAYA

THERE WAS A LATE END TO THE MONSOON IN 2002, which led to a poor success rate early in the postmonsoon season. Many of the successes were on the newly opened peaks, several of which are not as challenging or as high as the previously established list.

The confusing history of **Peak 41** (6,649 m) in the Khumbu at last reached the stage of an unquestioned official ascent. Due to an error in the coordinates specified by the Nepalese authorities, the frequently ascended and quite easy Mera Peak was confused with the much more difficult and dangerous Peak 41 about eight miles away. (See Alpina for June 2002.) Before and after the publication of the "error" there have been at least four unsuccessful attempts on Peak 41, two by the very well known Yasushi Yamanoi in 1998. At the end of September 2002 six Slovenians set up a base camp southwest of the peak. They then climbed Mera Peak for acclimatization and started up the W Face of Peak 41. Bad weather forced them down once, but on October 15,

Urban Golob, Matic Jost and Uros Samec headed up the 1,000-meter face again in cold weather and freshly fallen snow. Leaving at 3 A.M., they reached the crest of the N Ridge at a minor col and bivouacked. The next morning they climbed along the ridge to the summit, reaching the top at 9:30 A.M. on October 16. A second attempt by other expedition members reached the same col on the N Ridge, but was abandoned in a sudden storm. It is commonly and coyly said that this is not the first time that Peak 41 has been climbed; an illegal ascent by persons "known but unnamed" is credited.

In an attempt to sustain the tourist industry, much damaged by fears of terrorism, government instability, and the Maoist insurrection, the Government of Nepal has added more than one hundred new mountains and "Trekking Peaks"to the permitted list. Many of these are not particularly challenging (as Himalayan peaks go), fall into the class "peaks that no one has ever heard of," and may have been climbed unofficially or passed over on the way to something higher. Nevertheless, the first official ascent is a distinction, and the ascenders frequently encounter both the joys of pioneering and more difficulty than they anticipated. In the dubious weather of fall and early winter of 2002, the following were climbed: **Numri** (6,677 m) near Island Peak in the Khumbu, ascended on November 7 by Germans Olaf Rieck, Carsten Schmidt, and Lydia Schubert via the W Face; **Kyajo Ri** (6,186 m) north of Namche Bazar in the Goyko valley, ascended Oct 20 by Briton Duncan Wilson and Frenchman Vincent Marché via the SW Ridge; **Pokharkan** (6,346 m) NE of Annapurna near the Tibetan border, ascended by Koichi Kato and Sherpa Panima Lama on November 1 via the N Ridge and N Face; **Tangi Ragi Tau** (6,948 m) just north of the popular Tesi Lapcha pass, ascended by Koichi Ezaki, Ms. Ruchiya Takahashi, and two Sherpas on Dec 4 via the W face and S Ridge; and **Ombigaichen** (6,340 m) east of Ama Dablam, ascended by Charles Burr, Victor Saunders, and Sonam Yeltsin on December 5 via the S Ridge.

As usual, doubtful weather or not, there was a crowd up the easiest 8,000er, **Cho Oyo** (8,201 m); 28 expeditions placed almost 100 climbers on the summit. Most notable among these was Miss Toshiko Uchida who reached the top on October 1, aged 71 years and 172 days, thus gaining the title "oldest person to reach the top of an 8,000-meter peak ." The previous holder was the present Old Man of Everest, Yuchiro Miura, who was only 69 years and 209 days old when he climbed Cho Oyo in the spring of 2002.

On **Everest** (8,848 m) there were five postmonsoon attempts and one sad "success." Marco Siffredi, the young French snowboard expert, who made a descent of the Norton Couloir the year before, reached the summit on September 23 with three Sherpas via the N Col route. He intended to repeat his descent of the N Face using the Hornbein and Japanese Couloirs, and set off at 3 P.M. hoping to take only a little over an hour to reach a tent prepositioned on the Rongbuk glacier at 5,800 m. He was seen to reach about 8,600 m before 3:30 P.M., but no lower tracks were sighted, and no sign was found on the glacier below.

The 2003 season on Everest was, of course, the Commemorative Season for the fiftieth anniversary of the 1953 first ascent. In terms of the number of expeditions, climbers, hangers-on, and ascents it was probably the biggest season ever—but more conspicuous for ceremonial than for mountaineering accomplishment. See the article "Fifty Years of Climbing Everest" elsewhere in this *Appalachia*.

IN MEMORIAM. **Andrew John Kauffman II**, 1920–2003. Andrew Kauffman is best known to the international mountaineering community as a member (with Pete Schoening) of the summit team for the only American first ascent of an 8,000-meter peak—the ascent of Gasherbrum I (Hidden Peak) in 1958. There was a great deal more to his life than that. He had a successful career with the State Department and played a major role in the climbing, organizational, and literary aspects of American mountaineering. He was vice-president of the American Alpine Club, the American Vice-President of the Himalayan Club, and an Honorary member of the American Alpine Club and the AMC.

In the years following World War II, Kauffman with William Putnam was the major participant in the loosely organized and facetiously named "Colossal Enterprises," which mounted major mountaineering expeditions and provided many of the mountaineering articles in *Appalachia*, describing climbs from the second ascent of Mount St. Elias to the ascent of Gasherbrum. In fact, Putnam suggested to then-editor Miriam Underhill that Kaufman's account of the Gasherbrum ascent be subtitled "Colossal Enterprises Report from the Karakoram." She mentioned the suggestion but did not accede to it.

Probably the most important of his mountaineering publications was the study, together with Putnam, of the most controversial of American mountaineering disasters, the death of Dudley Wolfe and three Sherpas on K2 in 1939. The Kauffman and Putnam book, *K2: the 1939 Tragedy*, published in 1992, is a scholarly and courageous attempt to elucidate the complex series of events and to do justice to the participants, particularly Fritz Wiesner and Jack Durrance.

ACKNOWLEDGMENTS: These notes are based in part on accounts published in *High Mountain Sports* and the *American Alpine Journal*.

— **Jeffery Parrette**

News and Notes

AMC LAUNCHES MAINE WOODS INITIATIVE. Last December the AMC launched the Maine Woods Initiative, a bold new program for land conservation in the 100-Mile Wilderness region of central Maine. The conservation strategy will integrate habitat protection, recreation, education, and sustainable forestry in partnership with local communities, the state of Maine, forest products companies, conservation groups, and recreation organizations. The initiative seeks to address both ecology and economy in the Maine Woods region. In addition to protecting sensitive lands and retaining public access, it will support local forest products and recreation jobs, create new multiday backcountry experiences for visitors, and attract new nature-based tourism to the area. The initiative grew out of Vision 2010, a document developed in 2000 by the club's Board of Directors to frame goals for the next decade.

As a first major step in the program, the club announced the purchase of 37,000 acres of forest land, known as the Katahdin Iron Works (KIW) tract, from International Paper Co. (IP) for $14.2 million. The transaction was facilitated by the Trust for Public Land (TPL). The property is located between Moosehead Lake and Baxter State Park and surrounds the Little Lyford Pond Camps purchased by the AMC last June. With this acquisition, the AMC has protected a number of outstanding natural features, including the West Branch of the Pleasant River, a high-quality natural fishery, and a water source for the Gulf Hagas gorge; a 1,000-acre wetland complex, including a 300-acre bog; 25 ponds and lakes including Long and Houston Ponds; the spectacular Barren-Chairback Range; and Baker, Whitecap, and Little Spruce Mountains, the three highest peaks between Bigelow Mountain and Katahdin. The tract includes fifteen miles of the Appalachian Trail (AT) and is adjacent to Gulf Hagas and additional mileage along the AT.

"AMC felt compelled to act due to rapid changes in land ownership and growing recreational use," said AMC Deputy Director Walter Graff. "We have a once-in-a-lifetime opportunity to protect this area and broaden the range of options available for responsible backcountry recreation."

The AMC is developing a longterm management plan for the area, working with the state, local towns, and other environmental groups. To provide a basis for the plan, the club's Research Department is undertaking a thorough inventory of the property's ecological features. The plan will determine which areas will be managed for recreation, natural-area reserves, and sustainable forestry (the latter to be certified by a third party). New trails and a range of backcountry facilities will be considered. The club will work with local snowmobile clubs and the state on a plan to preserve popular snowmobile trails on the property and will honor leases held by several private sporting camps.

The AMC has a long tradition in the Maine woods. AMC members were the first to map Katahdin, and its crews built many of the early trails there. The Maine Chapter was established in 1956 and now has more than 3,000 members. The club has recently been active in other Maine recreation and conservation efforts as part of the Appalachian Trail Conference, the Northern Forest Alliance, and the Tumbledown Conservation Alliance. Last June the AMC and working partners completed the eastern half of the new forty-two–mile Grafton Loop Trail in western Maine, with the western half slated for completion in 2005.

Sources: AMC *Outdoors*; Maine Woods Initiative Press Release

AMC PURCHASES LITTLE LYFORD POND CAMPS IN MAINE.
In June 2003, the AMC added a new facility to its backcountry offerings when it purchased the Little Lyford Pond Camps near Greenville, Maine. The camps date back to the 1870s, when they were used as a base for logging operations, and have been operated as a traditional sporting camp since the early 1900s. When they came up for sale, the AMC took the opportunity to acquire a unique facility that will make new outdoor recreation opportunities available for its members and the general public. The camps are adjacent to the West Branch of the Pleasant River and the famed 100-Mile Wilderness on the Appalachian Trail. Several mountain peaks surround the 300-acre property. Recreation includes backcountry skiing, snowshoeing, hiking, paddling, and fishing on several remote ponds. Trails lead to nearby Gulf Hagas, known as "the Grand Canyon of Maine," and up Indian Mountain for views of the surrounding region. Facilities include ten rustic cabins with wood-burning stoves and gas and kerosene lamps, plus a main lodge where meals are served family-style. A cedar sauna is available for use in winter. Access is by car in summer

and fall, but in winter one must ski or snowshoe six-and-a-half-to-nine miles on an unplowed road to reach the camps. Arrangements can be made for transportation by snowmobile.

Sources: AMC *Outdoors*; Maine Sporting Camps, by Alice Arlen

AMC RECEIVES "EAR OF THE YEAR AWARD." In its year-end issue for 2003, the weekly *Mountain Ear* newspaper of North Conway, New Hampshire, named the AMC as the recipient of its 28th-annual "Ear of the Year" award. Since the paper's inception in 1976, the editorial staff has honored a person, event, or institution who has, in its view, "most contributed to the quality of life here in Mt. Washington Valley." The AMC was chosen for its long record of environmental stewardship and in celebration of the opening of the new Highland Center at Crawford Notch. A feature article cited the club's efforts in trail maintenance, mountain hospitality, outdoor exploration, scientific research, and environmental education, and also made note of the 125th anniversary capital campaign and Vision for 2010 plan, and the recent launching of the Maine Woods Initiative.

"And so, with this presentation of the 2003 'Ear of the Year' Award," wrote assistant editor Tom Eastman, "we hiking and skiing enthusiasts here at *The Ear* salute the AMC not only for its 127 years of stewardship, but also for its ongoing efforts in conservation, recreation, and education for generations of outdoor lovers in the years to come."

Source: *The Mountain Ear*, North Conway, NH (Tom Eastman)

GRAND OPENING FOR HIGHLAND CENTER. Hundreds of mountain lovers gathered last October 10 and 11 to help the AMC celebrate the grand opening of the Highland Center at Crawford Notch. The new environmental education center and lodge, located on the site of the historic Crawford House, opened its doors to its first guests last September. The weekend's activities included a grand-opening ceremony with comments by local officials, a local school teacher, AMC representatives, and world-renowned mountain explorers, Brad and Barbara Washburn. The weekend also brought the official unveiling of an exhibit of Brad Washburn's breathtaking mountain photographs on display in the center's Thayer Hall. The exhibit includes recordings of the Washburns commenting on the displayed photos.

As part of the celebration, the AMC presented U.S. Senator Judd Gregg (R-NH) with its first-ever Conservation Champion award, in recognition of his longterm leadership in the conservation of significant lands, rivers and natural resources in New Hampshire and across the region. AMC Executive Director Andrew J. Falender thanked Gregg for his "untiring efforts as a true steward of this country's special outdoor places."

Also joining in the celebration was U.S. Congressman Jeb Bradley (R-NH), fresh from a hike up his forty-sixth 4,000-foot peak in the White Mountains.

Other grand-opening events included a panel discussion on the creation and mission of the Highland Center and an open house with guided tours and displays on various AMC educational programs.

Source: Grand-opening press release

NEW ARETHUSA FALLS TRAIL OPENED. A reopening celebration for the Arethusa Falls Trail in Crawford Notch State Park was held on July 17, 2003 following a multiyear reconstruction project. The popular trail leads to the highest waterfall in New Hampshire, with a drop of nearly 200 feet. Over the years, the old trail to the falls had become washed out, rough, wet, and increasingly hazardous to use. The upper 0.8 mile has now been relocated farther up the slope, away from the brook, along the bed of an old logging road. The new footway is well graded, with many log steps and two footbridges spanning small brooks. At its upper end it meets the Arethusa-Ripley Falls Trail, which is then followed 0.2 down to the falls; the total distance from the trailhead is 1.5 miles. The project was a partnership involving the New Hampshire Division of Parks & Recreation, the Student Conservation Association, and AmeriCorps.

The falls were first discovered around 1840 by Dr. Edward Tuckerman. They were named in 1875 by guidebook editor Moses Sweetser and assistant state geologist Joshua H. Huntington, after a water nymph of Greek mythology featured in a poem by Percy Bysshe Shelley. The state of New Hampshire acquired the falls and surrounding land in 1930 through the efforts of AMC member Mary Peabody Williamson, a longtime guest at the nearby Crawford House.

Source: Program from reopening celebration

A SEGWAY TREK UP MOUNT WASHINGTON. The battery-powered human transporter known as the Segway has become the latest means of transportation used to ascend to the summit of Mount Washington. Last August a trio of riders took turns piloting the vehicle up the Mount Washington Auto Road, burning through six batteries during the eight-mile, two-and-a-half-hour journey.

Created by New Hampshire inventor Dean Kamen, the Segway was a media sensation when it was unveiled in 2001. The two-wheeled vehicle utilizes an intricate balancing system and is powered by both a battery and the forward leaning of the driver. On level ground, it can generally cover about 15 miles on a single battery charge, but with the 12 to 22 percent grade of the auto road, it was determined that multiple batteries would be needed for the ascent.

The three riders—Rob Owen, Dick Norris, and Steve Nickless—are all employees of the Heritage New Hampshire attraction in Glen, which also owns the Segway used for the climb. Owen began the trek at 11:30 A.M. and cruised for two miles up to an elevation of 3,000 feet. The first battery change was made here, and Norris took over the helm. The second battery was undercharged and lasted for a distance of just 1,000 feet. With a third battery in place, Norris continued the journey, emerging above treeline into wind gusts up to 60 MPH. As the grade steepened, the riders resorted to zigzag movements in a sort of uphill slalom to keep momentum going. At one point, Norris had to hunch over the handlebars and was brought to a stop for a second or two by the grade and the wind. "It brought me to my knees," he said. The last battery change took place only a few hundred feet below the summit. Owen took over for the last short leg and zigzagged to the end of the road just before 2:00 P.M. as onlookers cheered. Here he was presented with a bumper sticker reading, "This Segway Climbed Mt. Washington."

Source: *The Union Leader*, Manchester, New Hampshire (Lorna Colquhoun)

SPEEDING THROUGH THE HIGH PEAKS, PART II. In August 2002, Ted "Cave Dog" Keizer set a record for the fastest climb of the forty-eight 4,000-foot peaks of the White Mountains—3 days, 17 hours, 21 minutes (see *Appalachia*, June 2003). That standard stood for less than a year before it was bested by Tim Seaver, a 41-year-old Vermont hiker. From July 6–9, 2003,

Seaver turned in a time of 3 hours, 15 hours, 51 minutes for scaling the forty-eight peaks. He stashed water bottles at key points in advance of his marathon, and during the event he was aided by a small support team consisting of his wife Elisabeth and a few friends. Like Keizer, he slept for only short intervals along the trail or in the car between trailheads. He injured a tendon on Mount Cabot on the second day and intermittently suffered from a swollen and painful leg the rest of the way. Still, he managed to better Keizer's record by an hour and a half, finishing atop the remote peak of Owl's Head at 8:51 P.M. on July 9. His route covered 184.4 miles with 62,436 feet of elevation gain.

A new type of speed record was set during the early winter of 2003-2004 by Sue "Stinkyfeet" Johnston of Waterford, Vermont, and Bob "Frodo" Williams of Wilmington, Massachusetts. This pair of 38-year-old hikers made winter ascents of the forty-eight 4,000-footers in 10 days, 22 hours, 37 minutes, starting on December 26 and finishing atop Mount Waumbek early on the morning of January 6. No previous attempt had been made to establish a "Winter 4,000" speed record, though a handful of hikers had completed the list in one calendar winter. The variability of weather and snow conditions makes such attempts more problematical than summer "speed hikes." Heavy, fresh snowfall requiring extensive trail-breaking can slow even the strongest hiker to a crawl, while subzero cold and high winds can make above treeline-traverses unthinkable. Johnston and Williams's marathon excursion coincided with a period of relatively warm weather with little new snowfall, enabling them to complete the list ahead of their best-case scenario of 12 days. They still had their share of difficulties to contend with, including very icy conditions above treeline, rain, soft snow, high and unfrozen water crossings, and short daylight hours. The duo slept at friends' houses each night, though on their final day they hiked through the night, ending their quest at 5:37 A.M. The itinerary for that last day included Owl's Head, Mount Carrigian and Mount Waumbek—a total of thirty-nine miles with 9,500 feet of elevation gain.

Overall, Johnston and Williams hiked 227 miles (71 at night) with 71,000 feet of elevation gain and sixty water crossings; they broke trail in eight inches of snow or more on forty-five of the miles and did fourteen miles in the rain. They also made nine refueling visits to the Dunkin' Donuts in Lincoln. They were joined on many of the peaks by Thom Davis of Thornton, New

Hampshire, an original participant in the adventure who had to reduce his pace after sustaining an injury on the first day. Various other friends accompanied them on additional summits, though they hiked fourteen alone.

Johnston also holds the distinction of being the first woman to have hiked each White Mountain 4,000-foot peak in every month of the year, finishing in November 2003. To date, only four hikers are known to have accomplished the "48 X 12" feat, the others being Gene Daniell (co-editor of the AMC *White Mountain Guide* and former Accidents editor for *Appalachia*), Ed Hawkins, and Cathy Goodwin.

THE SEARCH FOR PATRIC MCCARTHY. One of the largest search efforts ever conducted in the White Mountains ended in sadness last October with the discovery of the body of Patric McCarthy, 10, of Bourne, Massachusetts. The boy became lost while playing in the woods with his stepbrothers between the Clearbrook and Village of Loon Mountain condominium complexes in the town of Lincoln. He was reported missing on the afternoon of October 13 (Columbus Day). The search was begun with tracking dogs and thermal-imaging equipment later that afternoon and continued through the night. The intensive effort continued for four more days under the direction of the New Hampshire Fish and Game Department, who utilized every available officer. Also involved were members of the Army National Guard and New England K-9 Search and Rescue. Each day, as many as 500 volunteers from across New England turned out to help with line searches through the woods. The area searched spanned from Lincoln Woods on the east to lower Franconia Notch on the west. The weather during the week included rain, wind, and nighttime temperatures in the 30s and 40s. On Friday afternoon a team of highly experienced searchers found Patric's body in thick growth, at an elevation of over 2,400 feet, high in the valley of Clear Brook between Whaleback and Big Coolidge Mountains, some 1,200 feet in elevation above the condominiums. Hypothermia was determined to the cause of death. Fish and Game officials were surprised that the boy had climbed so high up the valley over steep terrain and through dense growth. The search for Patric received widespread media coverage and touched the hearts of many across the region. The boy's family expressed heartfelt thanks to the hundreds who helped with the search.

Source: *The Union Leader*, Manchester, NH (Paula Tracy)

Editor's Note: We did not feel it was appropriate to place Patric's story in the Accidents section, but we also felt it was important to acknowledge this tragic mountain event, which reached many people across the nation.

More Land Conservation News

PONDICHERRY WILDLIFE REFUGE EXPANDED. The U.S. Fish and Wildlife Service has acquired 3,010 acres from the Hancock Timber Resource Group and has added it to the Pondicherry National Wildlife Refuge, located in the towns of Jefferson and Whitefield on the northern edge of the White Mountains. Pondicherry has been a refuge since 1964 and is a unit of the Sylvio O. Conte National Fish and Wildlife Refuge, which is managed by a partnership of the U.S. Fish and Wildlife Service, the Audubon Society of New Hampshire, and the New Hampshire Fish and Game Department. The Pondicherry refuge now includes just under 4,000 acres of protected land. The addition to the refuge received strong support from the communities of White-field and Jefferson, who worked closely with the Fish and Wildlife Service and the Audubon Society on the acquisition of the wooded acreage. The area will be open to the public for hiking, wildlife observation and photography, fishing, hunting, and environmental education. The refuge is well-known for its high-quality complex of bogs, ponds, streams and northern forest wetlands surrounded by boreal forest of spruce and fir. It is a designated National Natural Landmark. The centerpieces of the area are 100-acre Cherry Pond and 20-acre Little Cherry Pond. About 230 species of birds use the area during the year, with 125 species confirmed as breeding. In 2003 Pondicherry was designated as the first Important Bird Area in the state. The Sylvio O. Conte National Fish and Wildlife Refuge has its headquarters in Turner's Falls, Massachusetts and stretches along the Connecticut River valley from the Canadian border to the coast of Connecticut.

Source: Audubon Society of New Hampshire

PILLSBURY-SUNAPEE HIGHLANDS PROJECT. A $2.5 million federal grant has been secured to protect a large tract of forestland in the Pillsbury-Sunapee region in southwestern New Hampshire. The project was spear-headed by the Society for the Protection of New Hampshire Forests, with assistance in Congress from Rep. Charles Bass (R-NH) and Sen. Judd Gregg

(R-NH). The money was obtained from the Forest Legacy program. The state of New Hampshire will use the funds to acquire a conservation easement on nearly 7,000 acres owned by New Forestry LLC, a timberland investment company. The land is located primarily in the towns of Newbury, Goshen, Washington, and Bradford, with additional parcels farther north near Mount Cardigan State Park. Sustainable forestry will continue on the tract, while development will be prohibited and permanent public access for outdoor recreation required. The Society has secured easements or ownership on an additional 2,500 acres in the Pillsbury-Sunapee region. The newly protected lands will be added to the 25,000 acres, including Sunapee and Pillsbury State Parks, that already exist as conservation land in the region, making it the largest unfragmented forest block in New Hampshire south of the White Mountains.

Sources: The Union Leader, Manchester, NH (Paula Tracy); Forest Notes (Society for the Preservation of New Hampshire Forests)

MOOSE MOUNTAIN PROJECT. The U.S. Senate has appropriated $1 million of Forest Legacy funding to protect 4,200 acres in the Moose Mountain region of southeastern New Hampshire. The project is a cooperative effort involving the Society for the Preservation of New Hampshire Forests, Moose Mountain Regional Greenways, and the New Hampshire Fish and Game Department. The protected land is located in the towns of Alton, Brookfield, Middleton, and New Durham and provides important habitat for big-game species and threatened and endangered wildlife. It is adjacent to several tracts owned by New Hampshire Fish and Game. Also included in the 2004 appropriation is $1 million for land protection on the Lamprey River, a designated Wild and Scenic River in New Hampshire's fast-growing seacoast region; $250,000 for the Northern Forest Heritage Canoe Trail in northern New Hampshire; and funding for conservation of 12,800 acres in the Machias River ecosystem in Maine, for the final 7,700 acres of a 33,000-acre project around Tumbledown Mountain and Mount Blue State Park in Maine, for over 500 acres on Pochuck Mountain next to the Appalachian Trail in New York, and for 2,000 acres in the New Jersey Highlands on the Upper Delaware River watershed.

Sources: *The Union Leader*, Manchester, NH (Paula Tracy); AMC *Outdoors*

Guy Waterman Fund Awards
Alpine Stewardship Grants

Several projects aimed at educating visitors to the alpine zones of the Northeast received grants from the Guy Waterman Alpine Stewardship Fund in 2003.

The Green Mountain Club (GMC) received $2,500 for a "Reach and Teach" program that will teach alpine ecology to hiking groups, school groups, summer camps, and scout troops who frequently visit the Green Mountains. The groups will be contacted by GMC while still in the planning stages for their hikes, thus establishing partnerships and cooperation that will minimize visitor impacts once the hiking season begins.

The Dartmouth Outing Club (DOC) received $2,500 to launch a new summit steward program for the heavily visited alpine zone atop Mount Moosilauke. In cooperation with the White Mountain National Forest ridgerunner program, the DOC steward will educate hikers, do light trailwork, and help mitigate hiker impact on Moosilauke during the busy summer months.

With assistance from the Robert and Patricia Switzer Foundation of Maine, the Waterman Fund awarded $2,500 to the AMC to create an educational display for hikers visiting the extremely popular Franconia Ridge in the White Mountains. The display will inform hikers about the beauty and fragility of the alpine ecosystem and will be placed at the Lafayette Place trailhead.

Also in 2003, the the Randolph Mountain Club (RMC) completed construction of new weatherproof, bilingual signage at Crag Camp, the enclosed cabin perched on the edge of King Ravine in the Presidential Range. Instructions on caring for the alpine zone on the heavily visited slopes of the Northern Presidentials are printed in English and also in French to accommodate the large number of French-speaking visitors from Quebec. The Waterman Fund contributed $1,200 for the new signage, and RMC volunteers contributed money, expertise, and many hours of time toward the completion of the project.

Source: *The Alpine Steward*, newsletter of the Guy Waterman Alpine Stewardship Fund

—Compiled by Steven D. Smith

Books of Note

The Naked Mountain. Reinhold Messner.
The Mountaineers Books. 2003. 320 pages.

THE FIRST MAN TO CLIMB all fourteen 8,000-meter peaks, the first to summit Everest (with Peter Habeler) without supplementary oxygen, the first to solo to the top of Everest, Reinhold Messner has rightfully inspired awe among accomplished and armchair adventurers for more than three decades. But his most famous first—the summiting of his initial 8,000-footer, Nanga Parbat—remains the most talked about of his many exploits, because its achievement was marred by tragedy, blame, and lasting enmity. Messner made it back from the summit, exhausted, weak, and frostbitten—without his brother Günther, who died on the descent after following his brother to the top. What happened that day has been a source of debate within the mountain community since the 1970 expedition. Team leader Karl Maria Herrligkoffer claimed Messner was an opportunist who ran off to the summit alone in order to trump his companions and who ultimately sacrificed his brother to his own ambitions. *The Naked Mountain*, the ninth book by Messner that has been translated into English and published by The Mountaineers, is Messner's attempt to tell his side of the story and absolve himself of blame for an event that has, understandably, continued to haunt him. The book appeared in its original German in 2002 and reportedly heated up the arguments all over again. One can see why. Messner calls himself "the victim" of Herrligkoffer's manipulative behavior and unfounded accusations and makes serious accusations of his own about the motives of others involved in the expedition. Among other things, Messner says Herrligkoffer misled him about the weather and had decided before the trip who would get to the summit first. Saying in his introduction that memories from the long-ago experience remain "like a film in my head," Messner sets out to tell "the whole story in detail now, in order to include all those who are a part of what happened . . ." This is a stark read. Not only is the recounted experience harrowing in a deeply disturbing way, but the fact that it is a translation gives the prose a rather stilted, second-hand feel. More a polemic than a memoir, the book contains some sections that are actually written in point-counterpoint format. Messner's account will be most interesting to those who know the story of this expedition and its contentious aftermath or are willing to read other accounts to round out Messner's perspective. For those looking for a keen adventure story by one of the world's greatest climbers, it would probably be better to seek out one of Messner's other books.

—*Lucille Stott*

Sleeping Island. P. G. Downes. Prairie Books (Saskatoon, Sask.). 1988. 305 pages.

ASK WILDERNESS CANOEISTS to name their favorite book, and *Sleeping Island* is likely to be named more than any other. P. G. Downes lived in Concord, Massachusetts, taught humanities at Belmont Hill School, and spent his summers canoeing in the Canadian bush. For a review of his book, I can do no better than to quote from the back cover: "Sleeping Island is the sensitively written and moving account of one of his trips, a journey made in 1939 to the remote, and at that time unmapped, Nueltin Lake. Downes records a North that was soon to be no more, a landscape and a people barely touched by the white man. He described the excitement of wilderness canoe travel, the delights of discovering the land, and his deep feeling for the people met along the way. His respect for the Indians and the Inuit and their ways of life, and his love of their land, shine through throughout this richly descriptive work." And I would add, his quaint sense of humor. The book was first published in 1943. Here is a case where the newer edition is even better than the original, thanks to the extensive notes and fine photographs provided by the editor and historian, Robert H. Cockburn. I was about to shelve this review when I discovered to my dismay that the publisher has gone out of business. But Prof. Cockburn gave me the most welcome news: When Prairie Books folded, George Luste, realizing the great value of this superb edition, bought all of the remaining inventory of 200 copies. His Northern Books sells them for $25 postpaid while they last. Contact him at Box 211, Station P, Toronto, Ontario M5S 2S7 or norbooks@interlog.com.

—*Stewart Coffin*

The Hard Way: Stories of Danger, Survival and The Soul of Adventure. Mark Jenkins.
Simon and Schuster. 2002. 222 pages.

I READ THIS BOOK IN THE RIGHT MONTH of the right year: January 2004. In greater Boston's sea-girt region, the third coldest January on record, with average temperatures 8° below normal—a small ice age. On January 9 at 9:00 A.M. on Mount Washington, the temperature was −40.9°, the wind was gusting to 94 MPH, and the wind chill was approaching −100°. I had bookmarked this website of extremes, wondering if anyone might be abroad on the split rocks, seeking what adventure writer Mark Jenkins calls "The Hard Way."

Jenkins's book, a collection of column-length essays primarily from his work with *Outside* magazine, visits the expected difficulties, the heights and the narrows of the world. It contains storm and ice and surf; but it also takes us to swamplands and the unfurling margin of the road. It even probes the way foreign cultures can mimic weather, lining you up for exposure that can be lethal. But the book's essential tension is found in its framing: the prologue offers a brief description of leaving home—wife and daughters—for yet another adventure, this time in fractious Afghanistan; the final essay ("From the Mouths of Babes"), traces his daughters' second foray into climbing and the presence of Jenkins's now dead high-school swimming coach, the mythic spirit and teacher behind *The Hard Way*. Even for world roamer Jenkins, *The Hard Way* always bends toward the adventure of home and life at the core.

The writing in *The Hard Way* moves quickly and lucidly, sketching places, situations, and characters deftly. Because these are magazine columns, the development of thought is spare; in many instances, I wished for a longer exploration of the meaning of adventure. Such meaning is available, finally, in the accumulation of tales, but it struck me that perhaps the real promise of Jenkins's writing might be realized when the pace of his adventuring slows, and he spends more time sifting and combining a lifetime's search for the resilience that helps you learn who you are.

—*Sandy Stott*

Other books to consider:

River Otter: Handbook for Trip Planning. Maria Eschen. Anotter Press. 2003. 288 pages. A comprehensive guide for kayakers, canoeists, and rafters, this compendium of useful facts, checklists, group dynamics, safey and rescue techniques, and handy resources is a solid piece of work. Recommended for both new and experienced multiday water trippers.

Summit Strategies: Secrets to Mastering the Everest In Your Life. Gary P. Scott. Beyond Words Publishing. 2003. 128 pages. Gary Scott is a mountain guide who has led more than thirty expeditions in the Himalayas. An accomplished climber in his own right, he also served as general manager of the U.S. National Triathlon Team. Additionally, Scott is a professional speaker, and this little volume is a self-help book that uses mountain climbing metaphors to help readers think about personal goal setting, collaboration, and confidence building.

Mountain Climbing as American Transcendental Pilgrimage: Ralph Waldo Emerson and the Colorado 14ers Peakbaggers. Dennis Tobin. The Edwin Mellen Press. 2003. 234 pages. Dennis Tobin, Ph.D., is a scholar who studies the cultural geography of belief systems. This densely written book reads like a doctoral dissertation and so is not recommended for the general reader. We mention it here because parts of it might very well appeal to readers who relish the idea of connecting one of nineteenth-century New England's literary luminaries with the heights of Colorado. It includes interesting historical facts and intriguing connections between philosophy and landscape.

Origins: The Evolution of Continents, Oceans and Life. Ron Redfern. University of Oklahoma Press. 2003. 360 pages. Large format. Written and photographed by British science author Ron Fedfern, this beautifully wrought book draws on major discoveries about natural history, geology, geography, and paleontology to present a 700-million-year history of the earth. This isn't a book you're likely to read cover to cover, but it is a pleasure to delve into and would make a great gift for a student or teacher of earth science.

A Peak Ahead

A HIGHLIGHT OF OUR WINTER ISSUE will be a "Mountain Voice" interview with Fran Belcher conducted in March 1993, fourteen months before his death. One of Joe Dodge's many mountain disciples, Fran developed an early love of the AMC and would serve for nearly two decades—until 1975—as the club's first executive director. Besides being a devotee of the White Mountains, Fran was a scholar and a writer. This interview will allow him to share his rich experiences in his own words.

Also in our next issue, we'll join three novices in an ice-climbing class, run by International Mountain Equipment Climbing School Instructor Bill McKenna. The class, involving several climbs in Champney Falls, 20 miles from North Conway, New Hampshire, marked the last day of a ten-day mountaineering school. The twist is that two of the participants were male Plymouth State College students, and the third was a female professor. As you might imagine, that made for an interesting day.

Another essay will move us westward, to Camp 4 in Yosemite Valley. Along with a present-day hiking experience at the camp, this piece recounts the history of the place and cites the many noted climbers who have visited it over the years.

Please join us for these and many more high-country stories in the winter/spring *Appalachia*, which will appear in December 2004.

— Lucille Stott
Editor-in-Chief
stottdan@rcn.com

Submission Guidelines

Appalachia is a mountaineering and conservation journal published twice a year (June and December) by the Appalachian Mountain Club, 5 Joy Street, Boston, MA 02108. Non-profit. Format: 6 x 9 inches. Founded 1876. Circulation: approximately 14,000.

Editor-in-Chief: Lucille Stott. Poetry Editor: Parkman Howe.

Appalachia welcomes nonfiction submissions and queries on the following topics: hiking; trekking; rock climbing; canoeing and kayaking; nature; mountain history and lore; and conservation. We recommend reading a sample issue before submitting. Samples are available at the above address for $10 per copy (postage included). Please enclose a SASE with all submissions.

Poetry: Original poems about the above topics are also welcome. Shorter poems are preferred. Only eight poems are published per issue, which makes this the most competitive section of the journal; on average, one in fifty submissions is accepted.

Artwork: Photographs or drawings accompany most of our articles and are usually provided by the authors. We also publish a limited number of stand-alone photos that evoke the mountains and welcome high-quality freelance submissions.

Deadlines: Writers should submit unsolicited material no later than January 15 for the Summer/Fall issue, and no later than July 15 for the Winter/Spring issue. Because we publish only twice per year, writers should understand that accepted pieces might appear anywhere from six to eighteen months after acceptance.

Format: Articles generally run between 500 and 3,000 words and must be typed and double-spaced. Electronic submissions are welcome and may be sent to the editor in chief at: stottdan@rcn.com.

Editing: All work is subject to editing. We make every effort to review editing decisions with authors in the early stages of production, but deadlines make last-minute communication with authors impossible.

Payment: As a nonprofit journal, we cannot pay for unsolicited material. Authors receive two contributor copies.

Web publication: Excerpts from each issue are routinely published on AMC's website, www.outdoors.org, after the issue has been mailed.

WARNING!

Reading APPALACHIA'S accident reports could seriously improve your safety.

For more than 125 years **APPALACHIA** has been America's longest running biannual journal of mountaineering and conservation.

Subscribe today and you'll enjoy insightful stories of mountain adventure, conservation news, poetry, and the famous accident reports.

YES, I want to subscribe today!

❑ **$29 for 3 years ***special, limited-time offer***** (regular price $35 for 3 years)

❑ **$25 for 2 years**

❑ **$15 for 1 year**

Name _____

Address _____

City_____ **State**_____ **Zip** _____

E-mail_____ **Phone** _____
(if you would like to receive AMC information and updates)

❑ **Check enclosed** (please make check payable to APPALACHIA)
Charge my ❑ **VISA** ❑ **MasterCard** ❑ **AMEX**

Card number_____ **Exp date**_____

Call 1-800-262-4455 or visit www.outdoors.org